THE ÆSTHETIC
MOVEMENT & THE
ARTS AND CRAFTS
MOVEMENT. EDITED
BY PETER STANSKY
AND RODNEY SHEWAN.
FORTY-EIGHT OF THE
MOST IMPORTANT
BOOKS, REPRINTED IN
THIRTY-EIGHT VOLUMES.
GARLAND PUBLISHING, INC.

# ERNEST GIMSON
# HIS LIFE & WORK

 GARLAND PUBLISHING, INC.
NEW YORK & LONDON
1978

Bibliographical note:

this facsimile has been made
from a copy in the
Metropolitan Museum of Art Library
(120.32G42/Er6)

**Library of Congress Cataloging in Publication Data**
Main entry under title:

Ernest Gimson, his life & work.

  (The Aesthetic movement & the arts and crafts movement)
  Three articles on Gimson, with notes on the 60 plates.
  Reprint of the 1924 ed. published by the Shakespeare
Head Press, Stratford-upon Avon.
  1.  Gimson, Ernest, 1864-1919.  2.  Art industries
and trade--England--Biography.  I.  Series.
NK942.G5E7  1978     749.2'2 [B]     76-17779
ISBN 0-8240-2485-0

PRINTED IN THE UNITED STATES OF AMERICA

# ERNEST GIMSON

# ERNEST GIMSON HIS LIFE & WORK

Stratford-*upon*-Avon *at the* Shakespeare Head Press
London Ernest Benn *Limited* Bouverie Street
Oxford Basil Blackwell m.cm.xxiv

*Five hundred copies of* Ernest Gimson: His Life & Work
*have been printed in* England *at the*
Shakespeare Head Press Stratford-upon-Avon

*The Collotype Plates have been printed*
*at* Sussex House Hammersmith England *by*
Emery Walker *Limited*

*Number* 249.

# ERRATA

*Page* iv, *line* 1, *for* Five hundred copies *read* 550 copies.
*Page* 44, *line* 5 *from the bottom, for* Plate 39 *read* Plate 40,
    *and in the bottom line, for* Plate 39 *read* Plate 40.
*Page* 46, *line* 5 *from the bottom, for* Plate 53 *read* Plate 54.

# CONTENTS

## THE DRAWINGS IN THE TEXT

## THE PLATES IN COLLOTYPE

Contents

# ERNEST GIMSON'S LONDON DAYS

ERNEST GIMSON, having received his earlier training in an architect's office and at the Art School in Leicester, came to London in 1886 about the age of twenty-one. His chief teachers up to this time, that is his own elected prophets, were Ruskin and Morris, Auberon Herbert and Herbert Spencer. What he then was he remained, an idealist individualist. We used to argue about words, but ever felt—at least I did—that we meant the same things. The friends he first made in London were the brothers Barnsley, who came up nearly at the same time: Ernest a little before him to Sedding's office and Sidney a little later to Norman Shaw's. I had been with Norman Shaw since 1878 and in 1889 'set up for myself.' Alfred Powell went to Sedding's in 1887, and Robert S. Weir came to Shaw's in 1884. We all got to know one another very well, primarily because of the link the Barnsleys made between the two offices, but I had known Sedding from the time the Art-Workers' Guild was established in 1884.

Gimson came to see me in 1889, and from that time we were frequently together. In an old diary I find these entries:

1890. May 3. 'With Gimson to Sevenoaks and Knole. Stayed night at the "Crown," nice garden, walked back to Orpington in morning. Most lovely day—blue bells, violets & cherry-blossom. Talked of the necessity of keeping near to nature.' We visited the Priory House to see the delightful plaster frieze.

May 31. 'Perambulation with Gimson from West Wickham to Croydon.' Our objective was mainly the old alms-houses, then as now, I believe, threatened with destruction.

June 21. 'Walk with Gimson to Rickmansworth.' Another time we saw the great-roofed barn at Harmondsworth.

b

July 12. 'With Gimson to National Gallery and S.K. Museum.'
July 26. 'To Sevenoaks for a walk.'
August 2. 'Left for Holiday at Fountains Abbey with Gimson, stayed at Ripon the night.'
August 5. 'Drawing wallflowers at the Abbey: perfect day but feeling that it could not last.'
August 6. 'Letter calling me away, but walked to Pateley Bridge and back.' I returned to Fountains on the 9th and we remained until the 19th. We stayed at a farm called Hill House and had only a short walk through the home-field and down a wooded bank to the lovely grass flat where the grey old Abbey stands. I still remember the pinks growing from the crannied walls which we drew, and the story of a haunted house told by Mrs Brown. Her husband had had to ride past it one night for the doctor. 'Did he see anything?' 'No, but the horse did.' I remember too the skies: one seen on a moonlight night had a wonderful great cloud mapped out on it like a continent on an ocean, with gulfs & bays & lakes. It suggested looking at our own world from the sky. During the walk to Pateley Bridge to see a beautiful old pack-horse bridge for the 'Anti-Scrape' Society, we discussed the possibility of framing some satisfactory definition of 'Architecture.' We decided that architecture might bear some such relation to building as religion to morality, and then, borrowing Matthew Arnold's phrase as well as his general idea, we agreed that Architecture is building touched with emotion. I remember Gimson saying, 'I am thinking of architecture all the time I am awake.' Other entries in the same diary are:
October 24. 'Furniture shop scheme, meeting at Blomfield's in evening.'
November 15. 'Went down to Joldwynds [with Gimson] to see Philip Webb's house: liked it much.' These last entries will be explained further on.

Gimson had met William Morris at Leicester in his father's house, when Morris was giving a lecture there—probably in 1884. Morris I almost think suggested that Gimson should enter the office of J. D.

Sedding, which was next door to 447 Oxford Street, the headquarters of Morris & Co. at that time. When Gimson had been in London a few years he joined the Society for the Protection of Ancient Build-

## THE STROUD VALLEY FROM SAPPERTON

ings, which had been founded by Morris and Philip Webb several years before; I find his name in the list for 1890. Gimson became a keen & understanding member of the Committee, regularly attending the weekly meetings and visiting buildings in the Society's interest. Morris, as artist, made the profoundest impression on Gimson, and the Society was itself a remarkable teaching body. Dealing as it did with the common facts of traditional building in scores and hundreds of examples, it became under the technical guidance of Philip Webb, the architect, a real school of practical *building* — architecture with all the whims which we usually call 'design' left

3

out. Here we saw that architecture should mean solid realities, not paper promises, names and dreams. Here Gimson's love for old buildings deepened into a passionate reverence, and from this very regard he early came to see that ancient architecture was an essence & reality, not a 'style' which might be resumed in another kind of society at will by a different kind of people. It is a curious fact that this Society, engaged in an intense study of antiquity, became a school of rational builders and modern building. Here Gimson for years was in close contact with Philip Webb, Morris's friend from the Oxford days and for the early years of its existence the architectural member of Morris and Co.—a stern thinker and most able constructor.

It was Gimson who introduced me to the Society and the circle in 1891. For a time—a great time to me—we attended the meetings, from 5 to 7, and then went across the Strand to Gatti's for an evening meal: Morris often, Webb always, and two or three of a number of younger lesser people, Gimson, Emery Walker, Sydney Cockerell, Detmar Blow & myself; here were stories, jokes, and real talk. There was a kindly old waiter from North Italy whom we called Ticino, who smiled at us like a host.

At this time, about 1890, Gimson continued his own studies by visiting old towns and buildings in a quiet loitering way—his way —really looking at them and trying to understand, not taking rapid showy sketches and passing on in ignorance. I remember meeting, or visiting him, once at this time at Rochester: on going to his lodgings I found that he had brought with him large pieces of Morris chintz as an easy way of 'having something to look at' in his sitting room. There was no affectation in this, Gimson never had that, it was just an example of his quiet common-sense and knowing what he wanted.

In the study of old buildings most of us were visiting the great things of Europe, cathedrals and palaces. Gimson turned rather to more common & modest buildings of our own land, and these he not only thought pretty or picturesque, but he loved and understood them.

Understanding, as he now did, that art was *doing* not 'designing,'

4

he also set himself to learn some special crafts. These were in the first case modelled plastering, and a simple form of furniture-making. For the plaster-work he made an arrangement with Messrs Whitcombe and Priestley, who were doing the 'best domestic work' of the time. They appear before my memory as I write. Mr Whitcombe was puzzled by Gimson's 'messing about with plaster, dirty stuff,' but finally explained it as 'just his hobby.' The other craft was chairmaking. Gimson found that an old man called Clissett at Bosbury, near Ledbury, continued to make chairs in a traditional way: comfortable tall-backed things, parts were turned in a simple pole-lathe. others were shaped with a spoke-shave, and the seats were of rushes. These chairs had I think first been brought to London at the meeting-room of the Art-Workers' Guild. They were strong, light, shapely and entirely right. Gimson again apprenticed himself for a short term, and his intense interested intelligence soon mastered the art except for the quickness which comes of long practice.

I must quote a passage from Dr Mackail's *Life of William Morris* which excellently suggests the spirit which moved Gimson and his friends. 'What Morris himself had in earlier days done by the force of his own genius, was now being done on all sides with a conscious purpose. His own work in the early sixties had been based on two principles: the first that nothing should be done in his workshop which he did not know how to do himself; and the second that every form of decorative art could be subsumed under the single head "architecture" and had only a real life and intelligible meaning in its relation to the mistress art. Following on these principles, his pupils were now occupied in learning what they had to deal with in actual work at the lathe, or the dye-vat, or the mason's yard, and then in forming a really popular art. The Art-Workers' Guild, established in March 1884, had become an influence towards solidarity. But now an increased motive power might, it was thought, be given to the movement by public exhibitions of work done... The Art-Workers' Guild made the Arts and Crafts Exhibition Society possible. The project had taken form in the later months of 1887.' I forget whether

5

Gimson showed anything at the first exhibition in 1888, but at that held in 1890 he exhibited some admirable pieces of furniture. Mr Mervyn Macartney, Mr (now Sir R.) Blomfield and I also had pieces of furniture shown at the same time. Our interest in furniture-making at this period led to the formation of the (to us important) 'firm of Kenton & Company,' of which Gimson was certainly the most active spirit, because just at this time it was his chief interest. The note quoted above from my diary refers to a preliminary talk in regard to the formation of the 'firm.' The group interested consisted of Macartney and Blomfield; Gimson & S. Barnsley (who were now living together in Raymond Buildings, Gray's Inn); Colonel Mallet, a friend of Macartney's who 'had taste and knew people'; and finally myself. We each, I believe, put £100 into the business. Taking a workshop in some court north of Theobald's Road, we engaged an excellent foreman and wrote the name 'Kenton and Company' on the door. The name was taken from a street we passed through in going to the 'shop.' We enjoyed ourselves greatly for about two years, making many pieces of furniture, selling some at little over cost price—nothing being included for design or for time expended by the proprietors—and finally we divided up the remainder at the end by drawing lots for first choice. To my share fell what we still call 'the Gimson Cabinet' of walnut, 'left clean' and unpolished, but now mellow and glossy from use; another cabinet which we call 'Blomfield,' 'Barnsley's Table,' 'my Oak Chair,' and a little revolving bookcase designed by Macartney. After all, these five pieces with the fun and some experience gained were not a bad return for £100 down.

Gimson's furniture at this time and since was, it seems to me, one kind of 'perfect,' that is it was useful and right, pleasantly shaped and finished, good enough but not too good for ordinary use. As an example which may be seen by anyone I may mention the fine and specially ornate stalls of ebony inlaid with ivory in St Andrew's Chapel in the Roman Catholic Cathedral at Westminster. His furniture from the Kenton time, and increasingly when he had his own workshops and trusted men, was much more than his 'design.' Eve-

6

ry piece was thought definitely for particular picked woods and for clearly understood ways of workmanship, and his supervision was so constant and thorough that the design was changed in process of making as the materials and working might suggest.

His modelled plaster-work was entirely his own handiwork, and this was at least equally perfect. Plaster is in a way poor stuff, brittle and unpleasant to the touch; it must have been difficult to divine how it should be treated. Gimson saw some old work at Speke Hall, Haddon, Chastleton and Orpington, which suggested to his mind a technical method, and into that he at once put original adaptations from nature: rose, honeysuckle, pinks, lilies, strawberry plants and the like. I have before me a length of early frieze, a meandering stem throwing off roses & leaves. The distribution, type of relief and final expression are easy, masterly and just right, quite original and modern, but as good, every bit, as 'old work' and yet simple as piecrust. His affection—there is no other word for his likings—was ever for the measured and the modest. For instance he made a study of embroidery and drew some things for his sister: they were not peacock-hued splendours of silk but for white thread on white linen. In the summer of 1892 he carried out quite a large scheme of plaster-work in a house I was interested in. He lodged for months in a cottage close by, and after my visits to the 'works' in the morning we played cricket with the children in the afternoon. His building work was mostly done after the London days, but I well remember his plans for the house he himself built at Leicester. Already at this time he saw his building work through stone, brick, cob, and wood: his direct knowledge of two crafts gave him a sympathetic understanding of all, and always he kept within his strength; his works were not the sham grandeurs and vain ambitions of paper promises, but they were buildings. He drew beautifully in a tender Ruskinian way, but drawing was only with him a means, not an end in itself.

Philip Webb, our particular prophet, lived and had his office at 1 Raymond Buildings, in chambers overlooking Gray's Inn Gardens, the tall trees of which rose in front of the windows. Gimson and

7

S. Barnsley were naturally drawn there too and found most pleasant rooms at the end of 1890. There had been some talk before 'Kenton' was established of our joining in a sort of architects' shop, something outside the deathly dreariness of the respectable offices, with framed 'perspectives' on the walls and clerks slaving in the background, but it fell through—that is the shop did, but the perspectives and clerks never arrived for any of us. I went to 2 Gray's Inn Square, just opposite Raymond Buildings, in the spring of 1891, and for a year or two we were constantly 'in and out.' Then that old feeling that 'one must live near to Nature' came back to Gimson, and the end of the short London season drew to a close. He settled in a Gloucestershire village to produce as good work as might be and to get good work in kindred crafts done by others.

One of the deepest tragedies of death is the fact that it can never be known what they who have passed by were like, the love and appreciation of those who did know cannot be put wholly into words, and even the words are less in reading than in the writing. Only the echo of a memory or an opinion remains, and the work and the life itself too in some subtle way. Gimson had remarkable force; in this he reminds me of Morris, and like Morris 'he knew things' while still very young. Paper and prizes never misled him, 'design' did not worry him, he only wanted to do good work, or rather, for this is an ambiguous phrase in these days of 'brain labour,' he wanted to produce good *workmanship*.

His success was indeed wonderful, although it was but a tiny fraction of what 'might have been' if it could only have been understood what he was so able and willing to give. He obtained from ordinary country craftsmen results entirely delightful. And it may not be doubted that one of his chief aims, although he said little or nothing about it, was to bring back some pride and joy in work to the British working-man. His own craft of plaster-working he revolutionized, his experiments in it were comparable to those of Morris in printing. In his buildings he demonstrated that those who will build in pleasant ways, keeping near to the heart of the work and taking suggestions as it goes on, may attain results which are akin to those we all admire in old

8

STONEYWELL COTTAGE, LEICESTERSHIRE

work. All his work indeed, through being done simply and without any pretence of stylism, became like old work itself. Those who try to design 'in a style' necessarily produce something vastly different from the old, for theirs is not like the old work in its essential spirit but rather a copy of its superficialities.

Gimson was a thinker, an explorer, a teacher. I should like to say that I have known that of all the men of my own generation I might

ERNEST GIMSON'S COTTAGE AT PINBURY PARK

learn from him the most. That I have learnt I must not say, for that would imply some responsibility for my failures.

Most of all Gimson was a teacher who doubted words and spoke only in work. Work not words, things not designs, life not rewards were his aims.

W. R. LETHABY

# ERNEST GIMSON'S
# Gloucestershire Days

I ONCE heard a poet call himself a 'deep lover of the surface of the earth,' and it may with truth be said of Ernest Gimson that the secret of the excellence of his work lay in this same power of loving. Without it he never would have held such easy sway over all materials that came to his hand to be dealt with. It kept the edge on observation sharp and poetic and made arrogance impossible.

He was an individualist, but he did not force himself on his materials: as we know, his eye for inherent quality and his skill in developing it mark his work throughout. It was the same in the development of human qualities: 'Teaching is impossible; what we have to do is our own work, and let them see.'

He disliked setting materials to inappropriate use & protected his workmen from work he could not approve. The effect of work upon life was to him of far greater consequence than any purchaser's pocket. Some, who were unable to understand his purpose and ignorant of the sources of his power, were inclined to smile at his sequestered habit, for he chose to make his own traditions of life and work; but he was strong enough to cause strong men to doubt, and feel that he had in some way a firmer hold than they upon the essential things.

His outlook was always hopeful; he saw continually vistas that led to an ampler life, to a life of more real association for work and under better conditions. His enthusiasm seemed to increase with years, surviving all rebuffs and difficulties, and led him towards wider and firmer ideals. Sympathetic understanding found him always ready for explorative discussion of every kind of problem of art or manners. 'Politics' he never talked. He felt they did not lead anywhere, and he looked upon the whole business of it as a kind of game at blind man's buff.

His obvious & hearty enjoyment of the many things that touched

11

or interested him sprang of a mind always full and always close behind his cheerful countenance. At such times he had a peculiar look that I remember in no other face, of balanced intelligent pleasure at the point to overflow.

The constructive quality of his mind came out whenever he talked of any special work. His thinking was positive: to use an architecturalism, it was not sketching but drawing to scale, and when he used paper or pencil to explain or suggest he always used a rule as well and gave accurate dimensions, thus saving himself much time and effort. His purpose all through was construction more than mere suggestion; thought and materials were in close touch. He was safe and accurate: to watch him, or listen, convinced you that he was working from direct vision, and a drawing once made seldom needed revising or altering, but remained a clear statement of facts that had passed the careful scrutiny of his unerring common sense.

He came of a family that held long traditions of good handiwork, and his home was a centre for discussion of all kinds of interesting problems. He spoke to me once of the kind of talk he remembered listening to 'on matters of real moment' between his father and his father's friends.

It was when he was quite young that he met William Morris, and they seem to have known each other instinctively at once.

His mind was clearly made up on all questions of vital principle and never altered its main position. Similarly with his views and attitude towards religion, which were, as he said, temperamental.

He loved discussion and would always be ready to say what he felt or to listen to others: sometimes even to argue your point for you against himself.

He was not one to give up his position to ingenious or clever talk; but any illuminating truth he would be delighted to acknowledge at once; and he had that understanding and sense of proportion that belongs to all great minds.

All through his life he desired more than almost anything else to see a right beginning made in establishing good handicrafts and

12

GIMSON'S LIVING ROOM AT PINBURY

building in English country. He felt that there was no work of the revived arts in the world that could approach our own excellence and that to hand that on to a younger generation in a firmly established scheme would be the best thing that could be done for England. At one time, not long before he died, it seemed possible that a scheme would materialize, but owing to the war, and then his own health failing, the project must wait until, as he said, 'Some day the right people are sure to realize it.'

I remember him speaking once of the sheer inability of business wisdom among the commercially successful to understand good work and believe in it. On the other hand it would readily accept the 'make-believe' and push and establish that with avidity. To keep aloof from this commercialism he looked upon as 'our success, not our failure, as some seem to think.' He desired commercialism might leave handiwork and the arts alone and make use of its own wits and its own machinery. Let machinery be honest, he said, and make its own machine-buildings and its own machine-furniture; let it make its chairs and tables of stamped aluminium if it likes: why not?

He was very seldom bitter, but he knew his own worth, and the easy superiority of hard-faced business men provoked him at times to turn on their perversity. 'Can't you hear,' he said to me once, 'the scorn in their voices that says, "Oh yes, I know you, you artist fellows: you are very delightful," and so on, implying, as they finish, "but unable to do anything real, or carry anything through!" And just think of it, what we could and would do if they would let us!' As his friend W. R. Lethaby wrote of him, 'His success was wonderful, although it was but a tiny fraction of what might have been, if it could only have been understood what he was so able and willing to give.'

Architecture and building were the master interest of his life—sane dealing with the beauty of the earth, to make it a pleasantly habitable place for all wise and kindly people.

So professional architecture did not interest him. He wanted architecture full to the brim, and found this empty. He wanted it sincere, and found it full of strange habits; finally, he wanted it beautiful, and found it happily self-centred in 'making-believe.' Building customs, too, and traditions established through a thousand years were not, he felt, to be captured by a hundred years of science still on its trial.

Machine-work he looked upon as unreasonable in its demanding an output of certain kinds of energy out of all proportion to the pleasurable results.

Therefore, best building, as he understood it, was incompatible with professional practice, and he looked upon that practice as he would have done on any similar exploitation of arts—as comic in part, in part tragic, showing a people no longer desirous of exercising the whole of their faculties patiently to a reasonable end.

His own professional training was of the orthodox kind. He went through offices and came out with an ineffaceable impression that in that direction lay little hope for the growth of a live school of building craftsmen.

So we find him shaking off the dust of professionalism, exploring the architecture of England and Italy, filling books with measured pencil drawings, learning from the old men how they had expressed their pleasure in nature.

Returning to London he lived for a while with his friends Ernest and Sidney Barnsley, sharing rooms with the last named in Raymond's Buildings, Gray's Inn. Here his ideal began to show itself, and it was wonderful in old smoky London to find yourself in those fresh clean rooms, furnished with good oak furniture and a trestle table that at seasonable hours surrendered its drawing-boards to a good English meal, in which figured, if I remember right, at least on guest nights, a great stone jar of the best ale.

An attempt was made before quite abandoning London to carry on a furniture workshop as a way to being seriously occupied as artists, for it was impossible to regard professional architecture in that light. This went on for a time but was unsatisfactory and soon resulted in a determination to find a place in the country. That this decision was right the work subsequently done at Sapperton and at Daneway House is ample proof.

After much scouring of the country from Yorkshire to the South Downs the three friends found a home at Pinbury in Gloucestershire. The Cotswolds have become common knowledge since then; at that time they were a mystery land of difficult hills and deeply wooded valleys dividing the romantic Vale of White Horse from the Severn and the Welsh borderland. Pinbury lay some five miles to the west of the old market town of Cirencester, and practically the whole of that distance was, as it is still, covered with loveliest woodlands.

On the other side, a short half-hour's walk to the north and west took you into the heart of the Cotswold Hills, from whose uplands the estuary of the Severn, the Malvern Hills and the Black Mountains filled the western horizon.

Here in many a tiny valley, set there out of the rough winds and

15

## THE COTTAGE AT SAPPERTON: NORTH SIDE

driving snows of winter, were to be found marvellous stone-built farms, cottages and other small houses: their steeply gabled fronts making a lovely brightness in among the thick dark woodlands, or bringing the long grassy slopes of the limestone hills to a sharp finish with their 'picket ends' against the sky.

16

In those days Painswick was a stone village of the purest Cots- wold type: lying over its hill and round about its tall stone spire it was like an old city in miniature — stone-built, stone-tiled, and never a note of red to disturb its grey beauty.

Here then at Pinbury was promise of new possibilities in surround- ings that appealed to all the three friends. Every walk was a revelation of new wonders, and, satisfied & full of enjoyment, Gimson settled here for the work he was to do.

For twenty-five years he lived and worked at Pinbury and at Sapperton. Quietly his enthusiasm shaped itself, in building, in furni- ture-making, in plaster-work, and in ironwork; while socially in endless ways he was drawing together and invigorating whatever threads of true village life were still discernible.

It is to be remembered that throughout this time he was quite alive to the entire necessity to himself and his work of the country and of this Gloucestershire country in particular. Without it he could not have had half the power. He watched and he wondered — ab- sorbing everything around him. If you showed him any notable flower, or tree, or bird, or beast, he knew it well, and it opened his mouth to speak what was in him. So with books also. Wordsworth, for whom he was always ready, brought a brightness into his eyes, and opened the way for him to say things about nature and humanity — things he had spent his life considering. Wordsworth spoke to the child in him, and, as a friend who knew him long says, 'he always came out wonderfully to children.' He had a long bed of 'wild' daffodils beside the nut-walk at Pinbury which was one of the real delights of every spring. These things — the seasons, the flowers and all beside that grew and changed the earth — were intensely real to him. I never knew him to speak of them without a touch of music in his voice: he could not take them as a matter of course, and so it seemed that his flowers, his trees, his grass, were richer in association and more memorable than other people's.

Pinbury was a hill forming the head of one of the little Cotswold valleys. It had been nobly dealt with of old time by one Sir Robert

d                                                                                    17

Atkyns, and the Elizabethan house, now flanked symmetrically by enormous grouped sycamores and elms, planted there by him, stood towards the valley — gleaming white gables against the mass of foliage behind. Beneath the house the ground fell away to the valley — well covered with fruit trees in an orchard of thirteen acres, productive of many a pipe of cider, and along the crest of the hill ran the famous Nun's Walk, an avenue of ancient yews from sixty to seventy feet high. At midsummer the sun set in the central end of the vista, while at the eastern end a descent of stone steps led through a darkened stone gateway into the lower garden, square-walled and grass-pathed between its regular beds. A wall of twenty feet on the north of this garden was, as it were, the foundation of the old house whose gables showed atop of it. Here, round the house used and beautifully kept by Ernest Barnsley, was the front garden with the main entrance, a flagged path leading to the porch.

Behind the house on the west a farm building was converted by Gimson into a cottage, where he lived for six years alone & for nearly three years after he married. The room was large, and the floor flagged with white stone, the walls and ceiling, beams and joists white. A large black dresser, hung with gay and well-used crockery, a large settle at the fireside, and an oak armchair and other rush-bottom chairs made by himself on his pole lathe, were its furniture.

His love of Pinbury is hardly to be told. It could only be told in the slow way of the years & by the way he & his friends lived in it. Those who knew him best, knew it was made for him & him alone: it was a dream come true. A place perfectly architected & perfectly left alone, it held you entranced with its beauty: while the happiness of those that lived and worked there made it the one perfect colony of its kind.

There was nothing about Pinbury as he knew it of the country-seat: no display, no eccentricity. It was what a well-kept farm should be, easy of approach & a difficult place to leave, so broad and generous and easy was the welcome and the custom of it.

In 1903 Pinbury as a colony came to an end, and a move to Sapperton, a short mile away, followed, the three homes still neigh-

## THE COTTAGE AT SAPPERTON: SOUTH SIDE

bouring: one was an old cottage enlarged, one new-built, and his own also new-built of stone and high-roofed with straw thatch.

Helping him to set it out upon the ground, I could not but be astonished at the minute care and consideration given to the final placing, as if he had already lived in it and knew every requirement and every amenity of the house and its environment. Now with every passing year a maturer perfection grows upon his work, and though a little place 'tis greatly planned. Before leaving Pinbury came the permission from Earl Bathurst to make use of Daneway

House, the only almost untouched mediaeval Cotswold house left. Here were rooms well adapted for showing the furniture made in the adjoining workshops.

The house, dating from the fourteenth century and onwards, stands under a wooded hill, a tower with a four-gabled stone roof surmounting a tiny courtyard enclosed between the old hall and the later rooms added in the seventeenth century.

Much insight into his inner life was to be had at Daneway House among all his furniture. At the first glance all was of an extraordinary interest. Then one saw the beauty of the work: the substance, the development of the various woods, of the ivory, the silver, the brass, of inlays of coloured woods & shell. It was inevitable that you should find in the work now and then a humorous use of peculiar materials, an enjoyment of surprise; and for the work itself I have seen educated men & women, who might have been expected to behave differently, unable, short of actual laughter, to satisfy their delight in such perfect union of good workmanship with happy thought.

The reward of his life's work was coming rapidly even after the war, but I think his greatest pleasure was to know, as he did, that he had convinced so many of the real pre-eminence of good handiwork. His attitude towards his workmen was always the same, and he watched for their interests and was always planning and desiring to encourage them & give them his best. His knowledge & direction were in these days, to those of them that understood, a liberal education, and his chief smith said to me once that he found it hard to believe that Mr Gimson had not been a smith himself. So also spoke the plasterers in London while he learned their work with them.

Talking once of the cost of furniture-making and the price of it, he showed the kind of responsibility he felt towards those who worked for him by asking, 'What of the life-time of the worker? is he to be doing less than his best in order that someone may get a cheap article which may or may not interest him afterwards?' His tenacity of purpose all through his life and the impossibility of bending him aside from his chosen way drew him into a certain

20

loneliness that was yet not without grandeur. He prized any sign true sympathy and was utterly generous of all he had.

With all his strength he was highly sensitive, responding at once to any sincere appreciation of his work. He was in person tall and well built, with something more than a personality. It was personality of his spirit more than of his body, something that made the world look different, changing the standard, brightening, enlarging, appealing beyond the time and place. It is hard to say wherein he will be most missed by his friends. They cannot but feel that he has gone with his work only half done, another of the great Englishmen that we had but partly the wit to appreciate. It is the nation's loss that, however little noticed, will yet be found in the long reckoning. England is the better for him, and all who were privileged to be with him will long set their sails to catch the wind of his enthusiasm—his faith and fresh belief in England.

I would add these few notes of Ernest Gimson's life. Son of Josiah Gimson, an engineer, who died in 1883, Ernest Gimson was born in Leicester on the 21st of December, 1864. In 1881 he was articled to Isaac Barradale, a Leicester architect, with whom he stayed about three years.

In 1884 he met William Morris, and by him was introduced to J. D. Sedding, in whose office in London he spent some two years. Sedding's office was in Oxford Street, next door to Morris's shop.

After settling at Pinbury he married on the 14th of August, 1900, Emily Ann Thompson, daughter of the Rev. Robert Thompson, vicar of Skipsea in the East Riding of Yorkshire.

Together, first at Pinbury and afterwards at Sapperton their good will & ability & wonderful instinct made a home that he loved to live in, and one that can never be forgotten by any who enjoyed, not only its ready hospitality, but its quiet perfection and pleasurable ways.

In the midst of many works and much happiness of life he died, in his fifty-fifth year, on the 12th of August, 1919, and was buried under the yew trees in Sapperton Churchyard.

A. H. POWELL

# ERNEST GIMSON AND HIS WORK

THIS small tribute to the memory of Ernest Gimson needs an apology. My colleagues knew him throughout his working life, and their praise carries an authority in no need of support from such as mine. But although I am not qualified to say anything worthy of him and his work, and although I knew him only for a few years at the end of his life, yet those were years of friendship, during which we were much together—we were indeed for a little while working in partnership; and believing as I do that in his chosen sphere he was a great man whose untimely death robbed us of an example and an influence which were altogether for good, it may be possible for me to add something of use to this record, even if it should fail to do him justice. Nor can the plates at the end of this volume do his work justice; they can only convey an idea of what is called the design of it, which is only a small part of all that went to its making. However, there is a certain fitness in both these failures, at which he would have smiled in his kindly way, as if he had already warned us, because they bear out what he thought of our modern habit of writing about work, and of 'illustrations': he would say that work could be left to itself to secure all the notice and influence it deserved. On the other hand, the making of a book with a useful purpose, such as a record, and in the old ways of handiwork, would please him. And so, thinking of him, we have tried to make this one as he would have liked it if only for the sake of the craft. Moreover, we can point to examples of his work in public museums.

There can be no doubt, I think, that Ernest Gimson was a great creative genius, and in temperament and in all he did a very English genius. It may be against the fashion of the times to say this, but it ought to be taken into account in a review of his life & work, because

22

## DANEWAY HOUSE NEAR SAPPERTON

it has much to do with their character. Through much study he
became familiar with the long history of the English people, but
chiefly with the way they had lived and worked in times of peace
and how their various needs had been supplied. This interest was at
once social and artistic, and above all human. For him, art was so
interwoven with life that unless it had something to tell of the lives
of those who created it it was not good art, and life without art was

23

not normal. Let it be understood that he saw no great distinction between the arts and the crafts—the arts were the finer flowers of the crafts and not forced hot-house plants. Whether the crafts were of a cottage of the eighteenth century or of a church of the thirteenth, they gave him the same kind of pleasure. So it was that he had an especial love for the humbler ones, for they alone were an unbroken link with their golden period, the middle ages, having survived the renaissance, and (a much harder trial) many years of modern industrialism, even though they might not endure much longer. He held, therefore, that their traditions must be protected and developed under kindlier conditions, as the only means whereby we might hope to recreate a living national art.

This was the guiding impulse in his life's work. Art for art's sake or for luxury, or any art that did not minister to some human need, did not concern him—he found more to like in such as the make of an old lantern. It followed that in his affections old rural and domestic uses were as much linked with the craft as the craftsman himself. The elders of the countryside, their speech and customs, their songs, tales and memories, their opinions, especially of the changes they had seen forced upon them by the growth and activities of the great towns; their native conservatism, with its reverence for the ways of our forefathers, and its distrust of changes and very guarded acceptance of them as improvements,—in all these he saw, or rather felt, something with a meaning for himself, to which all his sympathies responded.

This meaning was that they had their roots in national, or regional, life and character, for these people had many things in common with our remote forebears, such as their love of nature and love of their own daily work when it might be honest and thorough; and, when their lot allowed, were reasonably contented, working, playing and singing as only happy people can, and as people did once when England was called Merry. He believed they were at heart much the same as their ancestors and with not very different needs; but he asked why it was that no one would call England either merry or contented now. He often talked of these things, and sometimes with hope.

It delighted him that beauty of the country (though little enough might be left to praise) was still, as it always had been, sung by our poets, and under the same impulse which still made cottage gardens trim and bright and sent children into the woods to gather flowers. He would say that not for nothing there lingered some repute for sound craftmanship, even in our factories. He saw no good in the flight of the younger country people to the big towns—it was only one more proof that England was suffering as from a disease which had marred her once lovely face, and was attacking her heart. Men might disagree about causes and remedies, but as to the need of cure there could be no doubt, the signs were too many.

These thoughts and cares brought Ernest Gimson into the company of men of a goodly succession: amongst whom he found his fellows and his friends. With these companions in the same quest, it became his great desire that his country should recover her old peace and contentment in her own ways, and to see to it that whatever he did was not unhelpful to that good cause. Like many of these men he came to think that what most needed mending could be called the conditions of work, for work, whatever the work was, meant far more than a means of livelihood. It could bring a man happiness as but few other things could, or it could degrade and do worse than make him miserable. Of course these truths were evident enough, but I think few things so angered Ernest Gimson as the idea that work at best must be dull toil, to be relieved and shortened by the machine as much as possible, in order that the worker might be free for play of the same vicarious kind. He held that work, and play as well, for each and everyone should be in some degree creative and responsible, because it was a need of man's very nature. When so employed his desires were fewer, and better; he would live not as a disruptive social unit but as a productive and peaceful citizen. Social security would follow with much good besides—not least, a return of that beauty in men's surroundings (so often mistaken for a cause

e

rather than an effect) which most of us desire and strive for to so little purpose now.

This ragged statement, I hope, fairly represents some of Ernest Gimson's opinions on a complex group of subjects. He was like William Morris in most of the ways each thought important, but he did not add precept to example as his great fellow and teacher did; I do not think he ever 'read' a paper publicly, or in any way published his views, so that they have to be reconstructed from memories of talks with him and from his letters. He would have wished them to remain unrecorded, as they might have been except that they help to an understanding of his life's work, and identify him with those whose labours he most admired. Thirty years ago William Morris said: 'Time was when everybody that made anything made a work of art besides a useful piece of goods, and it gave them pleasure to make it. That is an assertion from which nothing can drive me; whatever I doubt, I have no doubt of that. And, sirs, if there is anything in the business of my life worth doing, if I have any worthy aspiration, it is the hope that I may help to bring about the day when we shall be able to say, so it was once, so it is now.' And so with Ernest Gimson. He set before himself the same aspiration quite early in life, and he never looked back. It led him when, as a young man, he took the unusual course of leaving London, and all its 'prospects,' for good and all, to live in the country at Pinbury—a lonely and remote house— with his friends Ernest and Sidney Barnsley.

His instincts told him he would find survivals of old content and beauty where ancient traditions of life and work yet lingered: and these he found in one likeliest haunt, the valleys of Cotswold. Better able then, it was there he practised and perfected his skill in the crafts of building and furnishing. Before long he had built the house, between the village of Sapperton and his beloved Pinbury, where he spent the rest of his days, becoming more and more devoted to life there as the years went by, while his dislike of London or of any other such 'centre' grew to a loathing. I should never quite have known how real this was but for some visits to London with him, and two

26

journeys we had to make together through some of the northern cities to Stonyhurst College in Lancashire, where we were engaged in designing some memorial buildings. Usually he was the cheerfulest company, but as we approached the smoke & the squalid dwelling-rows of these cities he would shrink from the sight and become quiet and plainly unhappy. Once, when we had a long wait in Manchester, we spent the time over a tea-table in a corner (to which he had hurriedly dragged me, as if we were pursued) and surprised the waitress by shyly asking if we could be given 'something made in the country.'

His last visit to London was a short one, during the illness that proved fatal. We had taken him up to see the specialist from whom a hopeful verdict would have meant a longer stay and an operation; when we had returned the same afternoon to Paddington, he alone could smile—because he was not to stay in London, but could return to the country and his home for those last few days.

Of his work there is little that need be said; it is easier and better to agree with him & let it speak for itself. It is almost as much beyond praise as beyond criticism. With what he made for household use about one it is possible to feel as one should feel about such things: that they are for use and perfectly fitted for that use, that they are workmanlike and pleasing to look at, and there an end of it: so at least he would have wished these things to be regarded. Time was when a man might leave the 'taste' of his goods and chattels to those who made them, and mind his own business, as most people would prefer to do, one would think. I am sure he disliked that what he did should be thought of as 'decorative' or 'artistic,' and talked about in such a way. The few but wonderful examples of his skill in pure applied ornament are, one is tempted to say, in their proper places to-day in the museums to which most of them have gone. They prove themselves to be of true descent in the English tradition by a certain expression of preference for natural over abstract forms, more easily felt than described, but to be seen (to name examples) in the work of the mediaeval mason, and lingering in the same craft until the country mason of yesterday lost the last vestiges of free-dom, and in embroidery or needlework from the glorious days of *opus Anglicanum* to those of the samplers. His furniture seems now to be the best known of all his work, and even in the way of becom-ing famous,—not only, let us hope, because it must soon be rare,—but his iron and brass work was equally good, and might by their quality convince one that there had been no decline in the tradition, but that he had caught it at its best, and carried it on, so thoroughly did he succeed in these almost forgotten handicrafts.

There will be noticed in all his work a certain severity and purity of form; these followed the way he set about it. It is enough to say that this character can be seen and felt to be chiefly an expression of purpose, for quite clearly his 'design' for anything grew as natur-ally as an old house from the use to which it was to be put and the material from which it was to be made, as well as from his know-ledge of the craft and its traditions. Whatever there was of ornament came last, by way of joy in the work, from the rich storehouse of Nature which his windows looked upon, perfecting a beauty of the rare kind that endures. Of course in the use of this he was a consum-mate designer, but to speak of him as 'the greatest designer of furni-ture since Chippendale,' as has been done, implies a comparison, and is to fail to understand him, though the comparison would be instruc-tive. If he had designed in that way for the sake of ornament and dis-play, his great powers might have won for him a different fame—and the 'profits' he could ill afford to forgo. He chose, instead, a course wherein he believed others might more easily and usefully be led. In one sense he failed: his achievement, great as it was, falling short of his intention; for it was his fear that, after all, he had worked only in the modern ways of divided responsibility by designing work for execu-tion by other hands. He did at last see how difficult it was to hand on the threads of tradition he had found, and how difficult to coun-ter the influence set by to-day. But I think this was partly because those he taught, understanding how right he was, relied upon him as long as they might. He often spoke with regret of this, but never gave

28

up hope that he might one day obtain enough support to enable him to start a few craftsmen in the right way in their own shops.

Fortunately he is not lost as an influence. It may be a long time before work equal to his is made, and longer still before anything like it can take the place of the falsities and absurdities of to-day. Yet the time should come when workmen will decide the fashioning of their work in counsel with those who use it, and so end the evil of control by multiplied middlemen and shopkeepers, whose concern is their own profits, and in whose interests meanwhile we support follies like those of *l'art nouveau.*

Ernest Gimson was trained as an architect, and the few buildings to his name prove that he could have done as much for architecture as he did for his chosen crafts, and perhaps a great deal more. The pity is that opportunity was denied him—an old story in the history of the arts. He liked to tell of the way he would set to work on some great hall or church, or even a barn (like William Morris he loved barns), but in the end he had built nothing but the library & hall of Bedales School and a few small houses. Again and again he seemed well started on something worthy of himself, and with renewed joy would throw into it all his energy and knowledge (and what a force they were!) only to see it all brought to nought. Not one of these designs was not a masterpiece. Yet many were rejected, and in favour of something really bad, and then it seemed that here was something too good to be realized to-day. Still he remained patient and hopeful, & if he thought himself neglected or underrated he never shewed it. In dealing with his clients he was tireless in his efforts to please them, within the limits set by his principles, and not impatient in listening to opinions that hindered him.

It will be understood that in building, as in his other crafts, his 'designs' were not drawn to look well on paper. The purpose of the building was kept before him, the site carefully noted, local labour and materials and their traditional usage studied, and then followed —not a mimicry of any bygone 'style,' but something of to-day, so honest and natural, so familiar to the ground and welcome to the site, that it was, as it were, of local family and descent. It soon looked as if Nature herself had taken a hand in maturing it, and a good deal 'older' (as in truth it was) than the 'Gothic' and 'Jacobean' houses of yesterday. I heard a visitor once ask him the age of his own house, expecting to hear a history. 'Let me see,' he replied, 'it must be nearly seventeen years old.' There was an excuse for the question,—modern houses do not look like that. Yet there was nothing old in the room except a clock and a few books and such like, nor anything that pretended to be old. Newly cut stone and oak, bright steel and glass, and white walls reflecting the sunshine— nothing was there but for use and comfort, and all without any sort of make-believe. Yet it looked 'old.' Turning to ask oneself why, one read the answer in those sturdy materials in use as our forefathers through centuries had learned to use them and remembered anew that those ways are not our ways; that they are too good and 'not good enough' for us; that we have changed them all; and that nothing has so disfigured the face of England as that change. Not to speak of speculators and jerry-building, good materials would seem now to matter less than 'style,' or stylishness—to be had in a 'wide range' of choice advised by the expert in 'taste.'

Once, when Ernest Gimson was finishing a house, the builder said to him, 'What do I think of it now? Well, sir, in my opinion, it's a great deal too countrified.' Annoyed that this was so merrily taken as a compliment, he added, 'Well, I am thankful to say, our next job is for a real London architect.' Ernest Gimson was fond of the little story, and it helps one, as it helped him, to understand why his work was so little wanted.

It is difficult to leave the subject of his work without a word of regret that he had so few opportunities. His crafts often brought him nothing but unnecessary labour & annoyance & only latterly were not a cost to him; the greater part of his labour in plans for building was thrown away. Yet these were losses cheerfully borne in that unflagging pursuit of his ideals which signed his greatness. Regrets such as these are ours rather than they were his. His energy and cheer were renewed like the

30

## SAPPERTON CHURCHYARD

morning, and his daily work in itself brought its own ample reward
His life was one of deep and sober happiness, for he had a way of
seeing and enjoying the good in everything. Of his pleasures there
were few to equal those he found in nature, except the fireside joys
of his home and the part in village life he shared with his wife. In

all these he carried everyone with him. To accompany him in his 'daily walks and ancient neighbourhood' was to learn and be delighted, and one could not but feel something of his love of the birds and flowers, of which his knowledge seemed inexhaustible. In all the village pastimes he was the leader, and the youngest; no merrymaking or dance went half so well without him; when he led the Twenty-Ninth of May there were no idle feet. With his wife he taught Sapperton how to 'enjoy itself,' and it will be long before those happy lessons are forgotten there.

To say as much about him and his work without some reference to Ernest and Sidney Barnsley, his friends from first to last, and to Norman Jewson, his pupil and friend of later years, would be wrong, and would have hurt his generous heart. They were a part of his life, and their almost daily intercourse must have been a mutual help and encouragement, of value to him as to them, which he, no less than they, would have acknowledged.

His most enduring visible mark at Sapperton will be his house and garden. They may long retain the beauty that only he could have given them; but the ineffable charm of the life they first saw has gone. There were the happiest work and play, music and laughter, with recaptured peace and leisure, at such a distance, as it seemed, from to-day that all its discords were silenced. There he died, and thence he was carried to be laid in the spot he would have chosen.

Much is lost with him, but the greatest loss is not for those who mourn him, but for that England of his hopes in whose service he spent his life, and for whose sake, no less than by virtue of his own great qualities of heart and mind, he left the world, it can truly be said, better than he found it.

F. L. GRIGGS

# THE DRAWINGS IN THE TEXT

These drawings are all by F. L. Griggs, A.R.A., except that of the interior of the cottage at Pinbury Park, which is by Alfred H. Powell.

## THE STROUD VALLEY FROM SAPPERTON     Page 3

THE cottages in the foreground are among the oldest in the village. The view is that from the Village Hall, in which Ernest and Mrs Gimson taught the villagers Morris, Sword and Country-Dancing, produced simple country plays & in many other ways added to the healthy enjoyment of the villagers.

## STONEYWELL COTTAGE, LEICESTERSHIRE     Page 9

A DRAWING of the cottage built for Mr Sydney A. Gimson in the Charnwood Forest. See also Plates 2, 3, 16.

## ERNEST GIMSON'S COTTAGE AT PINBURY PARK     Page 10

THE cottage in which he lived is shewn in the immediate foreground. At that time the cottage was detached from the old house, part of which is seen beyond. The central portion, with the stone bay window and gable over, was added soon after he moved to Sapperton and contains the carved stone mantlepiece & modelled plaster ceiling shewn on Plates 54 and 55.

## GIMSON'S LIVING ROOM AT PINBURY     Page 13

THE drawing shews the interior of the living room as it was when Ernest Gimson lived there.

f                                                                         33

**Drawings**   GIMSON'S COTTAGE AT SAPPERTON: NORTH SIDE
Page 16

THIS drawing shews the dormered thatched roof, high chimney stack, rounded projection for the staircase and the open shed with the dormer windows of his workroom over.

GIMSON'S COTTAGE AT SAPPERTON: SOUTH SIDE
Page 19

THE drawing shews the wide flight of steps from the garden up to the entrance on the higher level and the beech-trees beyond the cottage. See also Plates 5, 16.

DANEWAY HOUSE, NEAR SAPPERTON     Page 23

THIS beautiful old house, part of which dates from the 14th century with later additions mostly of the 17th century, was rented from Earl Bathurst. The large stable buildings were adapted to form workshops for the cabinet-workers, and in the house itself were shewn furniture made in the workshops and metalwork made by the Sapperton blacksmiths.

SAPPERTON CHURCHYARD     Page 31

HIS grave is under the yew-tree near the gate of the churchyard. The tombstone is of Edgeworth stone, with the inscription cut on a copper plate fixed to the stone, a traditional local type of memorial. The old tombstones in the foreground are of the same type.

# THE PLATES IN
# COLLOTYPE

THE plates have been made from drawings by Ernest Gimson and photographs of his completed work. Many of the plates are from his actual working drawings, in some cases shewing signs of handling in the workshops or on buildings, as the case may be, but it has been thought better to reproduce them in the condition they were left in at his death, with all his rough notes and instructions on them, rather than to make any attempt to tidy them up in any way for the sake of a little added clearness.

The drawings and photographs selected for reproduction have been chosen from a very large number of almost equal interest, many having only been omitted owing to the necessity of limiting the number of plates. It is therefore hoped that individual subscribers will not be disappointed at the omission of plates illustrating particular works in which they are interested, but will recognize that his friends have done their best to ensure that the plates shall worthily illustrate his work in all its branches.

The photographs of Rockyfield Cottage and of the stalls in Westminster Cathedral have appeared in *Country Life* and are reproduced by permission of the Editor.

Those on Plates 1, 2, and 4 (1) are by Mr Harold Baker of Birmingham, those on Plate 6 by the late Mr Blackburn of Budleigh Salterton, those on Plates 8 and 11 by Emery Walker Limited (by whom also the Collotypes were made), and that on Plate 38 (6) by Mr Newton of Leicester. All the rest of the photographs are by Mr Dennis Moss of Cirencester.

35

PLATE 1 (1). A HOUSE IN LEICESTER. *Built for himself in* 1892.

AS the photograph shews, this is a simple straightforward building, like all Gimson's work entirely free from definitely 'architectural' features, but relying for its effect on good proportion and the sympathetic use of good local materials.

The walls are of Leicester sand stock bricks with wide flush joints, and the roof is covered with the beautiful many-coloured slates which at that time were still quarried in the Charnwood Forest at Swithland and Groby.

(2). WHITE HOUSE, LEICESTER. *Built for Arthur Gimson, Esq., in* 1897.

THE walls of wire-cut bricks, specially made so that the sides and ends of the bricks were cut with the wires to give a rougher texture, flush-jointed and lime-washed. The chimney-stacks of red sand stocks and the roofs of Swithland slates. A bay window on either side of the house is rough-cast, with panels modelled *in situ* in cement.

PLATE 2 (1). A PAIR OF COTTAGES NEAR MARKFIELD, LEICESTER. *Built for James Bilson, Esq., in* 1897.

THIS pair of cottages near Markfield, Stoneywell Cottage and Lea Cottage, were built at the same time in a very beautiful part of the Charnwood Forest, a district which he had known and loved from boyhood. The hard local rock, outcrops of which abound in the heath and woodlands of the district, was used for the walls of all these cottages, undressed by the tool, thick pieces of slate from the disused quarries being used over door and window openings. Mr Detmar Blow, who had gathered together and trained a band of skilled masons, was responsible for all the walling, and no one else could have carried out Gimson's intentions so skilfully and sym-

36

pathetically as he has here done. The constructional timber used for all these cottages was English larch, worked by Richard Harrison & Sons, the Sapperton wheelwrights. Strap hinges, latches and such other ironwork as was required were made by the Sapperton blacksmith. The windows were glazed with crown glass.

For Mr Bilson's cottages the roofs were covered with Swithland slates.

## (2). STONEYWELL COTTAGE. *Built for Sydney A. Gimson, Esq., in* 1898.

THE plan of this cottage was determined by the outcrop of rocks on the site, these being used in lieu of foundations as far as possible. The intractable nature of the rock used for building and the consequent ruggedness of the walls can be clearly seen in the photograph. The roof is thatched.

## PLATE 3. STONEYWELL COTTAGE. *Some of the working drawings.*

THE sections shew the careful working out of all the constructional details. The timber was converted and all curved and other members selected and worked under Gimson's constant supervision. Comparison between the elevation and the photograph on the previous plate will shew how faithfully the spirit of the drawing was interpreted.

## PLATE 4 (1). LEA COTTAGE. *Built for Mentor Gimson, Esq., in* 1898.

ONE of the same group and built of similar materials but with the walls lime-washed.

## (2). ROCKYFIELD COTTAGE. *Built for Miss Margaret Gimson in* 1908.

A LATER addition to the same group of cottages, built of similar materials by a small local builder.

37

PLATE 5. ERNEST GIMSON'S OWN COTTAGE AT SAPPERTON. *Built in* 1903. *Two working drawings*.

THE walls are of limestone quarried on the site, with dressings of Minchinhampton Common stone. The constructional timbers and joinery are of larch and oak locally grown, and the roof is thatched with wheat-straw. The thatcher was John Durham, of Fifield, Oxfordshire, a splendid craftsman, now unfortunately unable to do further work.

PLATE 6. A COTTAGE AT BUDLEIGH SALTERTON. *Built in* 1912 *for G. Basil Young, Esq*.

THE walls of cob, a material which had then practically gone out of use, though more or less successful efforts have since been made to revive it. At the time the cottage was built, a few local men knew how to build in cob, and Mr Young, who acted as his own clerk-of-works, persuaded them to put their knowledge to good use. The roof is covered with 'reed' straw thatch, and the timbers and joinery are of English oak and chestnut. In view of the material used it is interesting to note that this cottage, apart from all work to the garden, cost less than 6d. per foot cube.

PLATE 7 (1). UPPER PORTION OF A WINDOW FOR WHAPLODE CHURCH, LINCOLNSHIRE.

THIS Church was repaired by Mr W. Weir, of the Society for the Protection of Ancient Buildings, and the necessary work included replacing the missing tracery of this window. As it is contrary to the principles of the Society to 'restore' tracery in stone imitative of old work, thus falsifying the history of the building, it was decided to fill in the vacant space with tracery in English oak which in construction and detail would necessarily differ from any stone tracery. This work having been entrusted to Gimson, he evolved the design shewn, and it was carried out in his workshops at Daneway House.

38

(2). SCREEN IN ENGLISH OAK FOR A CHURCH
AT CROCKHAM HILL.

THIS modern Church was altered in 1918, Earl Ferrers being the architect responsible for the alterations. The screen was designed by Ernest Gimson, and with the exception of the subject panels, which are the work of Mr George Jack, it was carried out at the Daneway House workshops, most of the work being finished before his death. The work was finished and fixed under the superintendence of Mr P. Waals, his foreman.

PLATE 8. HALL AT BEDALES SCHOOL, NEAR PETERSFIELD, HANTS.

BUILT in 1910 for his old school by Mr Geoffrey Lupton, at one time a pupil at Daneway House. The walls are of local hand-made bricks with wide flush joints, the roof of hand-made plain tiles, and all woodwork in English oak.

PLATE 9. THE COTTAGES AT KELMSCOTT.
*Built in 1915 for Miss May Morris.*

BUILT near the Manor House, where William Morris, whose life and example meant so much to Gimson, had lived. These cottages are built with walls of the good grey stone, and roofs of the stone tiles of the district and with English larch timbers, in every way as Morris would have loved, had he been alive to see them. Walter Gissing, an old pupil, afterwards killed in the war, acted as clerk of the works.

PLATE 10. TUNLEY HOUSE.

DRAWINGS made in 1913 for a house which he had intended to build on a site he had bought at Tunley, between Daneway and Edgeworth. The house was never built.

39

PLATES 11, 12, 13, 14. BEDALES SCHOOL WAR
MEMORIAL BUILDINGS.

TWO photographs and details of the Library and some of the
drawings for the complete scheme. All the drawings for the
Library and the small-scale drawings for the complete scheme were
completed some months before his death, and at his request Mr
Sidney H. Barnsley superintended the subsequent carrying out of
the work. Up to the present, funds have only permitted of the building of the Library, now practically finished by Mr Geoffrey Lupton.
The materials are local hand-made bricks for the walls, hand-made
tiles for the roof and English oak for all timber & joinery. The casements and other wrought ironwork were made by S. Mustoe, one
of the smiths formerly employed at Sapperton.

PLATE 15. FAIRFORD WAR MEMORIAL CROSS.

THE design for this Cross was the last work that he completed. It was intended that the Cross should stand in the
centre of the Market Place, but owing to considerable local opposi-
tion to the use of this site the War Memorial Committee decided to
place it in the Churchyard, where it was erected in 1919 under the
superintendence of Mr Norman Jewson.

PLATE 16. PLANS OF THE BUILDINGS SHEWN
ON THE PREVIOUS PLATES.

# NOTE ON THE DANEWAY HOUSE WORKSHOPS

THE cabinet-work shewn in the following plates was all made
in the workshops of Daneway House. Mr Peter Waals, the
foreman, had been trained in Holland and acquired further knowledge of his craft in other Continental workshops before coming to

London, where Gimson found him. Of the other cabinet-makers the nucleus came from London, and afterwards local boys were apprenticed and trained to the work.

Gimson at first made the turned chairs himself, using an old pole lathe. Later they were made by Edward Gardiner at the Daneway saw-mills.

PLATE 17. WORKING DRAWINGS FOR AN ALTAR CROSS, in black ebony inlaid with ivory and red coral.

MADE for St Peter's, Vere Street, W., as a Memorial to Keith Debenham. A pair of candlesticks in ebony and ivory also formed part of the memorial.

PLATE 18. DRAWING FOR AN ALTAR CROSS, in ebony, inlaid with silver and mother-of-pearl. Made in 1912.

PLATE 19. TURNED CHAIRS IN YEW AND ASH. Working drawings.

PLATE 20. DESIGNS FOR CHESTS OF DRAWERS, veneered and inlaid with holly & ebony and with hand-made brass handles.

PLATE 21. LARGE DRESSER IN ENGLISH OAK. Working drawing.

PLATE 22. DESIGN FOR A LECTERN IN EBONY. Inlaid with ivory, mother-of-pearl and silver.

A FIRST sketch and photograph of the complete work. The candlesticks are of polished wrought iron. The lectern was made in 1906 for Roker Church.

PLATE 23 (1). A CHEST IN ELM AND EBONY. (2). A CHEST IN ENGLISH WALNUT. Inlaid with darker walnut and cherry, on a stand of English walnut, with hand-made brass drawer handles.

PLATE 33. A SINGLE SEAT MADE IN ENGLISH WALNUT. Inlaid with bone. Made as a model for the stalls in St Andrew's Chapel, Westminster Cathedral.

PLATE 34 (1). A BISHOP'S THRONE & CLERGY SEAT. In Cuban mahogany. For Khartoum Cathedral.
(2). STALLS IN BROWN EBONY. Inlaid with bone. For St Andrew's Chapel, Westminster Cathedral.

PLATE 35 (1). A LECTERN IN BROWN EBONY.
(2). A LECTERN IN ENGLISH OAK.
(3). A CLERGY SEAT IN ENGLISH OAK.
(4). A CLERGY SEAT & DESK IN ENGLISH OAK.

PLATE 36 (1). A CHAIR IN BURR-ELM VENEER AND EBONY.
(2). TWO CHAIRS IN ENGLISH WALNUT.
(3). AN ARM-CHAIR IN ENGLISH OAK.
(4). A CHILD'S CHAIR IN ENGLISH WALNUT.
(5). AN ARM-CHAIR IN ENGLISH WALNUT.

PLATE 37. CHAIRS IN TURNED ASH WITH RUSH SEATS.

PLATE 38. SETTEE & CHAIRS IN TURNED ASH WITH RUSH SEATS.

PLATE 39 (1). A BOX IN EBONY. Inlaid with ivory and palm.
(2). A BOX IN EBONY & MOTHER-OF-PEARL.
(3). A BOX IN ENGLISH WALNUT. Inlaid with walnut and bone.

43

PLATE 39 (*continued*)

(4). A BOX IN ENGLISH WALNUT, with mar-quetrie of walnut and cherry.

(5). AN EBONY BOX. Inlaid with sections of mutton bone with centres of cocoanut shell, the knob and feet of jade and silver, by Paul Cooper.

(6). AN EBONY BOX, with inlay of ivory and silver. Original in the Leicester Museum.

# NOTE ON METALWORK

THE metalwork illustrated, as well as the brass & iron handles and latches for cabinet work & also a great deal of architectural ironwork, such as strap-hinges, latches, casements, wrought-iron gates, &c., were made by Gimson's own smiths in his black-smiths' shops at Sapperton. None of the blacksmiths had had, before he engaged them, any special training for the highly skilled work required in much that was produced. Frequent technical difficulties had to be overcome, as well as the determining of the right finish for each piece. A great deal of his time was consequently spent in the shops, which he visited almost every day.

PLATE 40. FIRE-DOGS. Working Drawings for two pairs of pierced, chased and slightly embossed fire-dogs in polished wrought iron. One of these designs was also carried out in brass.

PLATE 41. FIRE-DOGS. Photograph of one pair of fire-dogs made from the design shewn on Plate 39.

PLATE 42 (1). CANDLE SCONCES. Photograph of two candle sconces in brass, pierced and engraved.

(2). FIRE-DOGS. Photograph of the other pair of fire-dogs made from the design shewn on Plate 39.

PLATES 43, 44, 45. SCONCES. Working Drawings and one preliminary sketch for sconces for candles and electric light, those on Plates 42 and 43 in brass, on Plate 44 in polished wrought iron.

PLATE 46. WROUGHT IRONWORK. Working Drawings for polished wrought-iron latches, handles and bolts. (A tracing from one of his original drawings.)

PLATE 47. WELL-HEAD. Working Drawing for a well-head in wrought iron for Old Place, Mochrum, Wigtonshire.

PLATE 48. ALTAR CANDLESTICKS. Design for altar candlesticks, 4ft high, for Hopesay Church, in chased and pierced brass.

PLATE 49. TABLE CANDLESTICKS. Design for a pair of table candlesticks in polished wrought iron.

PLATE 50 (1). WEATHERCOCK. Working Drawing for a weathercock in brass gilt. Part only shewn.
(2). A FIREGUARD in polished wrought iron.

PLATE 51. A STAND OF FIRE-IRONS in polished wrought iron.

PLATE 52. AN ALTAR CROSS in pierced, chased and polished wrought iron, 3ft high, for Roker Church.

# NOTE ON PLASTERWORK

PLASTERWORK was one of the first crafts which Gimson took up and one in which he afterwards constantly worked. As in all he undertook, Gimson first obtained a thorough grasp of the possibilities and limitations of the material he was going to work in and then based his practice on the knowledge so acquired. He

45

used soft rounded forms and avoided all undercutting, in complete variance with the methods then in vogue, though this manner of working has since become familiar through his example and influence.

The ceilings shewn in the following plates are selected from a large number, for all of which he modelled fresh patterns.

PLATE 53. TWO CEILINGS in modelled plasterwork.

PLATE 54. INTERIOR OF A ROOM at Pinbury Park, shewing stone mantle-piece, fire-dogs and modelled plaster ceiling, all by Ernest Gimson.

# NOTE ON GIMSON'S WORK IN OTHER CRAFTS

BESIDES his work in Architecture, Cabinet Work, Metalwork and Modelled Plaster, Gimson made a number of designs for Stone and Wood Carving, Embroidery and other crafts. The following four plates were chosen from among a great many working drawings of such things in order that this side of his work should not be entirely unrepresented.

Most of his designs for Embroidery were made for his sister, Miss Margaret Gimson, while the designs for Bookbinding (including a complete set of tools) were made for his sister-in-law, Miss Ethel Thompson.

PLATE 55. MANTLE-PIECE. Working Drawing for stone carving on the mantle-piece shewn on Plate 53. The drawing has been traced over by the carver.

PLATE 56. EMBROIDERY. First sketch for a design for an embroidered hanging.

PLATE 57. SAMPLER. Design for a sampler in cross-stitch.

PLATE 58. BOOKBINDING. A book bound by Miss Ethel Thompson, the cover designed by Ernest Gimson: 'The Gospels from the Prayer Book, for use at High Mass.'

# NOTE ON EARLY DRAWINGS

THE following two plates reproduce three of the many drawings which he made during his student period.

PLATE 59. A DRAWING made in 1889 of one of a pair of fire-dogs at Haddon Hall.

PLATE 60 (1). A DRAWING made in 1888 of stone carving at the Church of St-Trophime at Arles.

(2). A DRAWING made in 1890 of a 13th-century wall painting, 'The Wheel of Fortune,' on the North side of the Choir of Rochester Cathedral.

Plate 1

1. A HOUSE IN LEICESTER   (Plan on Plate 16)

2. WHITE HOUSE, LEICESTER   (Plan on Plate 16)

Plate 2

1. COTTAGES NEAR MARKFIELD (Plan on Plate 16)

2. STONEYWELL COTTAGE, MARKFIELD (Plan on Plate 16)

Plate 3

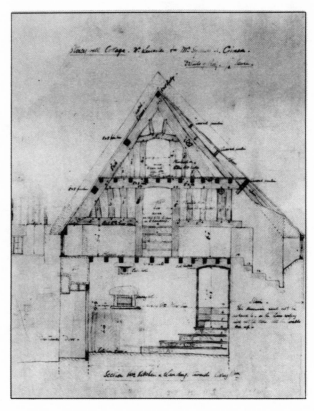

DRAWINGS FOR STONEYWELL COTTAGE   (Plate 2)

Plate 4

1. LEA COTTAGE, MARKFIELD (Plan on Plate 16)

2. ROCKYFIELD COTTAGE, MARKFIELD (Plan on Plate 16)

Plate 5

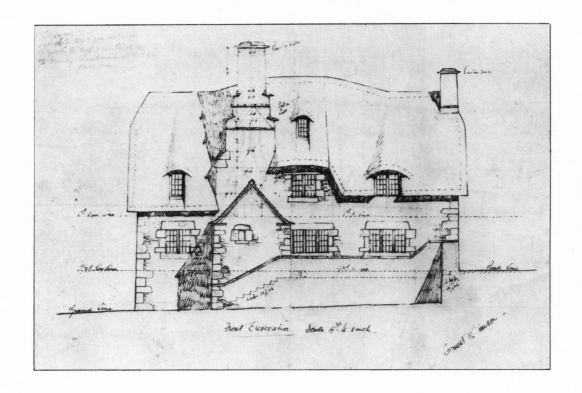

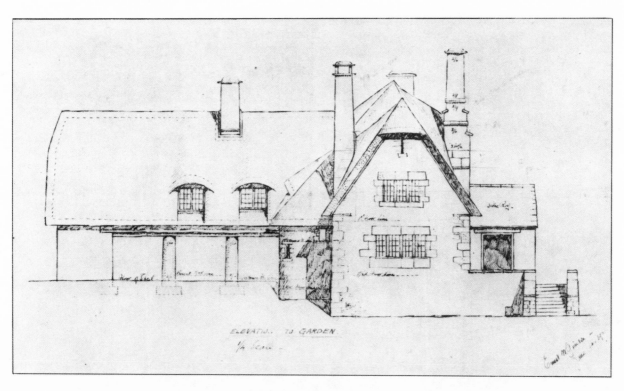

**COTTAGE AT SAPPERTON**   (Plan on Plate 16)

Plate 6

COTTAGE AT BUDLEIGH SALTERTON   (Plan on Plate 16)

Plate 7

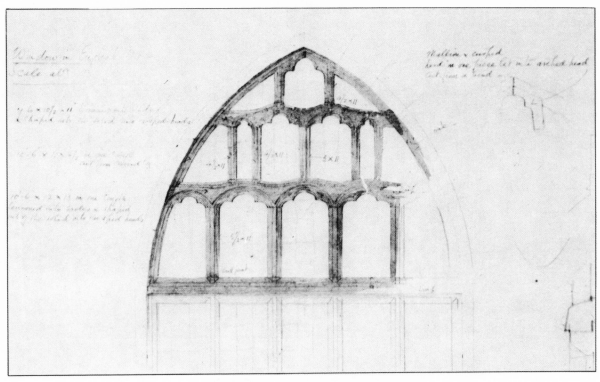

1. WINDOW AT WHAPLODE CHURCH

2. SCREEN AT CROCKHAM HILL CHURCH

Plate 8

HALL AT BEDALES SCHOOL   (Plan on Plate 11)

Plate 9

COTTAGES AT KELMSCOTT   (Plan on Plate 16)

Plate 10

·NORTH·ELEVATION·

·SOUTH·ELEVATION·

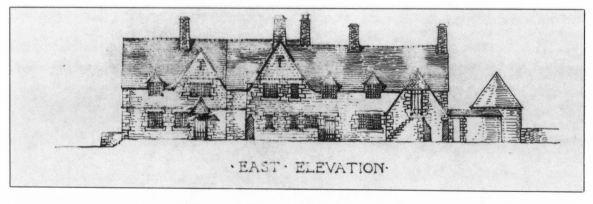

·EAST·ELEVATION·

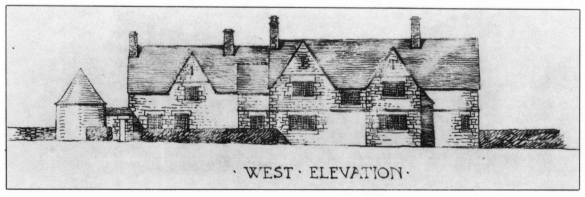

·WEST·ELEVATION·

**TUNLEY HOUSE**  (Plan on Plate 16)

Plate 11

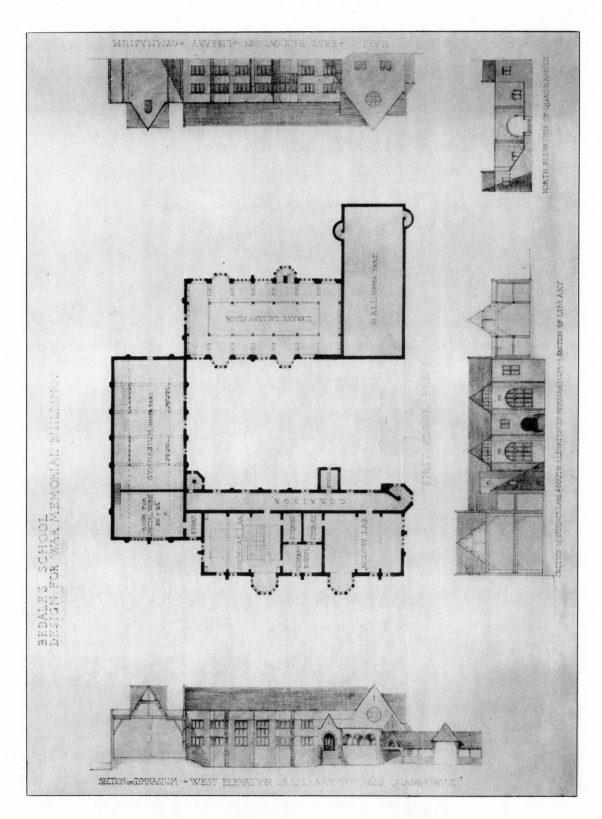

BEDALES SCHOOL. DESIGN FOR WAR MEMORIAL

Plate 12

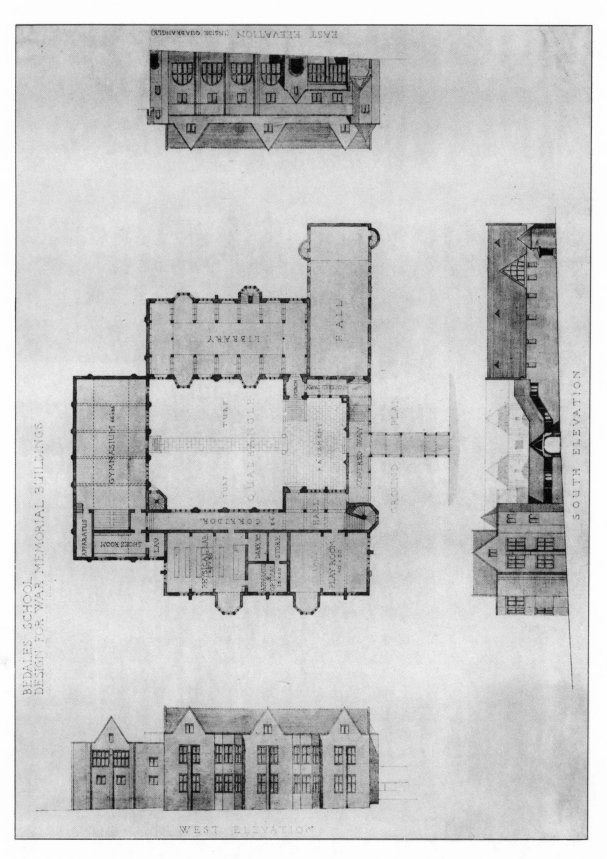

BEDALES SCHOOL. DESIGN FOR WAR MEMORIAL

Plate 13

BEDALES SCHOOL WAR MEMORIAL. THE LIBRARY

Plate 14

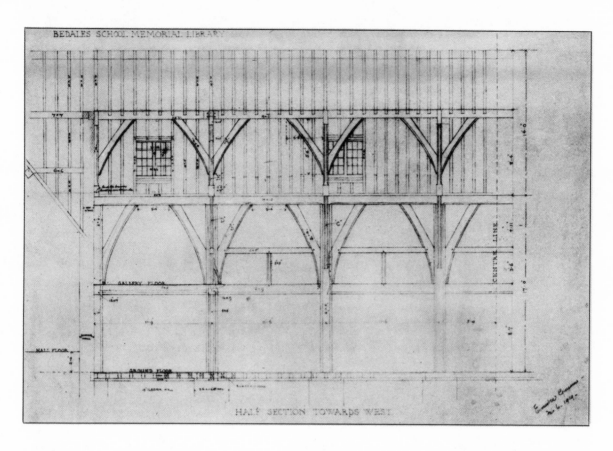

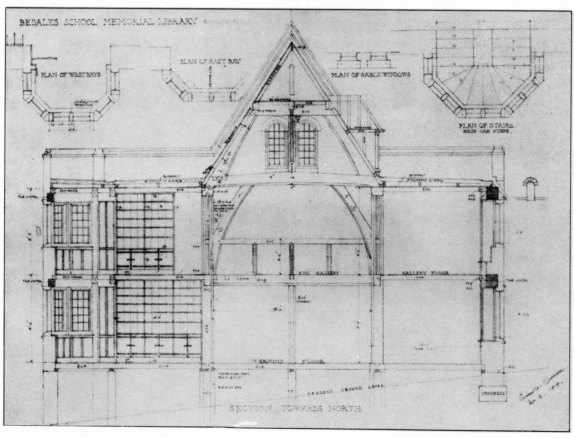

BEDALES SCHOOL WAR MEMORIAL. DETAILS FOR THE LIBRARY

Plate 15

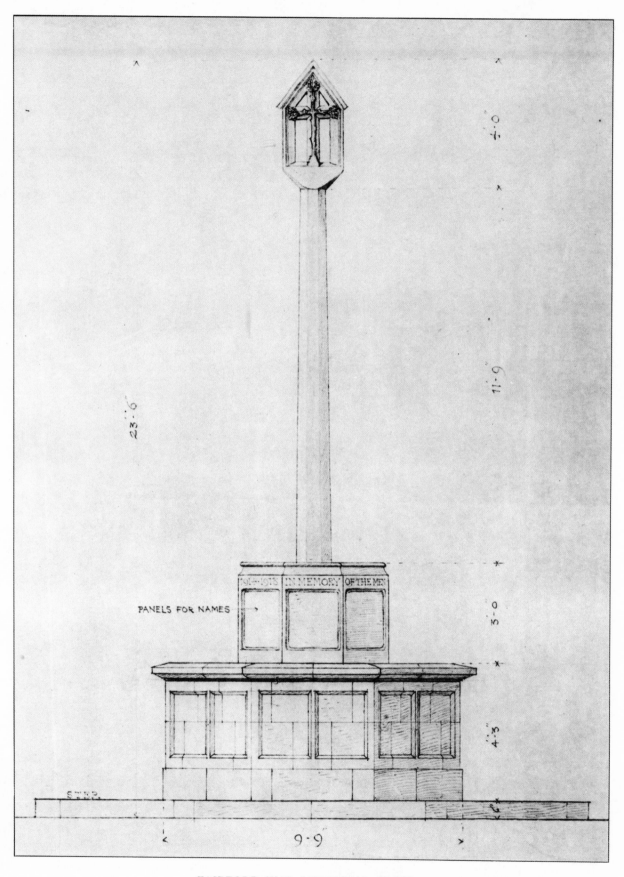

PANELS FOR NAMES

FAIRFORD WAR MEMORIAL CROSS

Plate 16

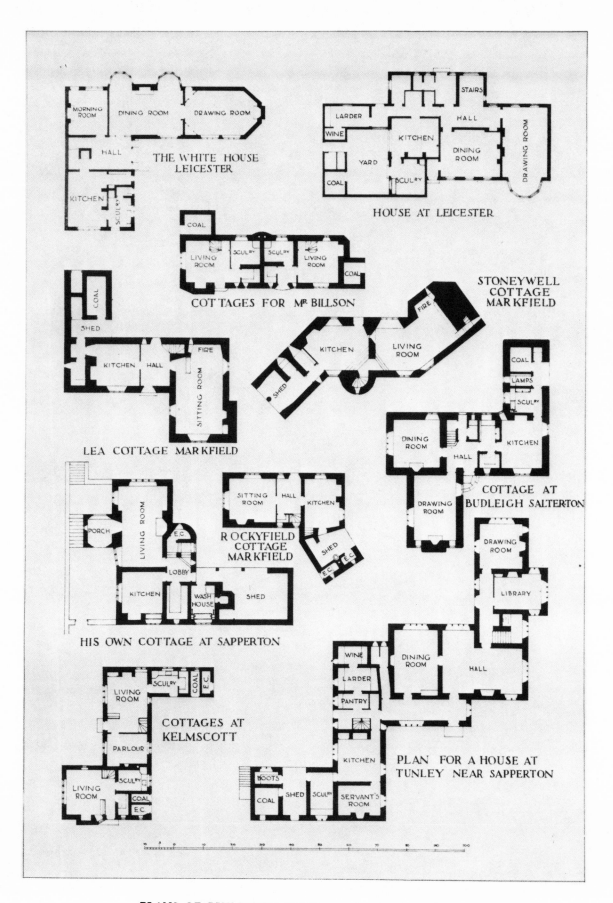

THE WHITE HOUSE
LEICESTER

MORNING ROOM · DINING ROOM · DRAWING ROOM
HALL
KITCHEN · SCUL&sup;RY

HOUSE AT LEICESTER

LARDER · WINE · COAL · YARD · KITCHEN · SCUL&sup;RY · STAIRS · HALL · DINING ROOM · DRAWING ROOM

COTTAGES FOR M&sup;R BILLSON

COAL · LIVING ROOM · SCUL&sup;RY · SCUL&sup;RY · LIVING ROOM · COAL

STONEYWELL COTTAGE MARKFIELD

FIRE · SHED · KITCHEN · LIVING ROOM

LEA COTTAGE MARKFIELD

COAL · SHED · KITCHEN · HALL · FIRE · SITTING ROOM

COTTAGE AT BUDLEIGH SALTERTON

COAL · LAMPS · SCUL&sup;RY · DINING ROOM · HALL · KITCHEN · DRAWING ROOM

ROCKYFIELD COTTAGE MARKFIELD

SITTING ROOM · HALL · KITCHEN · SHED · E.C. · E.C.

HIS OWN COTTAGE AT SAPPERTON

PORCH · LIVING ROOM · E.C. · LOBBY · KITCHEN · WASH HOUSE · SHED

DRAWING ROOM · LIBRARY

COTTAGES AT KELMSCOTT

LIVING ROOM · SCUL&sup;RY · COAL · E.C. · PARLOUR · LIVING ROOM · SCUL&sup;RY · COAL · E.C.

PLAN FOR A HOUSE AT TUNLEY NEAR SAPPERTON

WINE · LARDER · PANTRY · DINING ROOM · HALL · KITCHEN · BOOTS · COAL · SHED · SCUL&sup;RY · SERVANT'S ROOM

PLANS OF BUILDINGS ON Plates 1, 2, 3, 4, 5, 6, 9 and 10

Plate 17

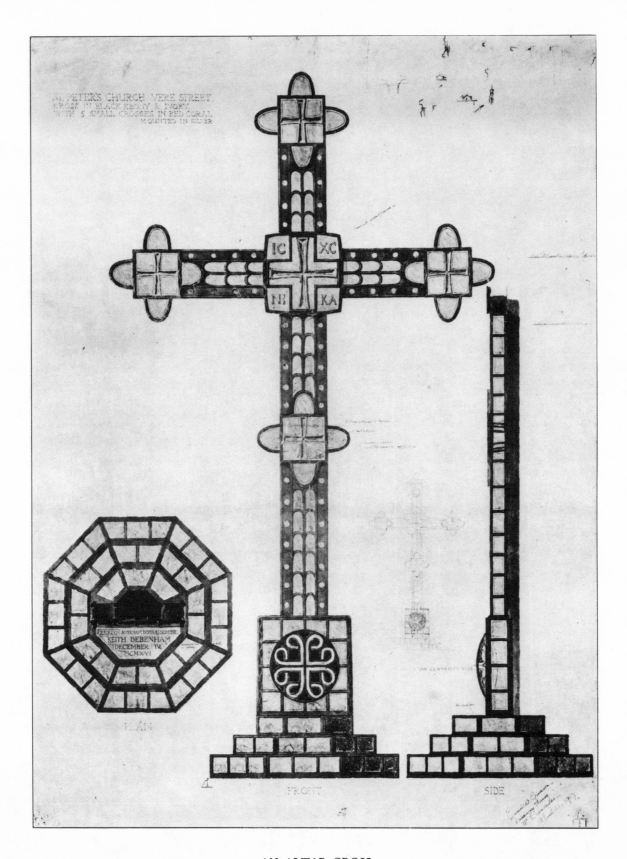

AN ALTAR CROSS

Plate 18

AN ALTAR CROSS

Plate 19

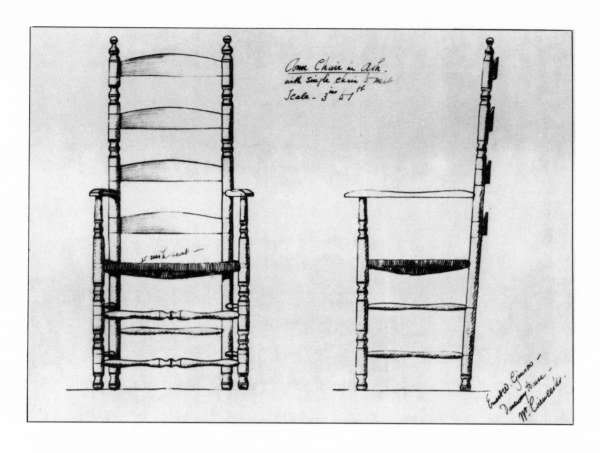

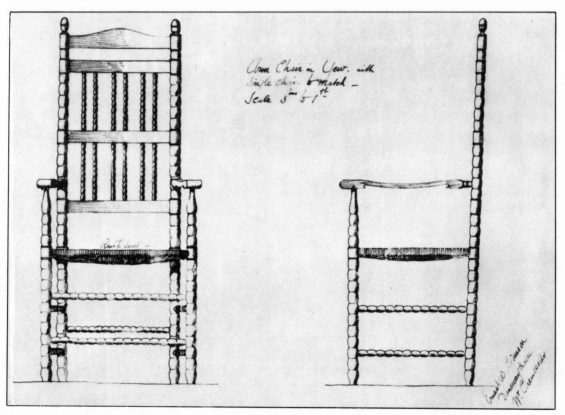

**TURNED CHAIRS**

Plate 20

CHESTS OF DRAWERS AND CABINETS

Plate 21

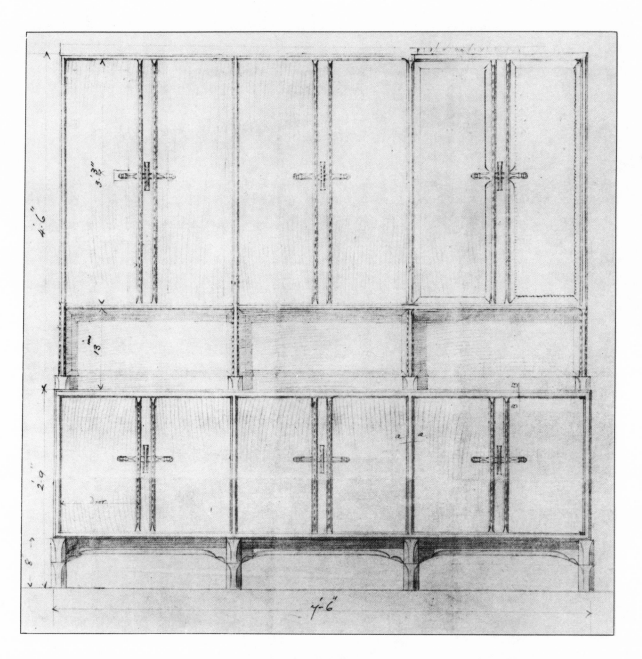

A LARGE DRESSER

Plate 22

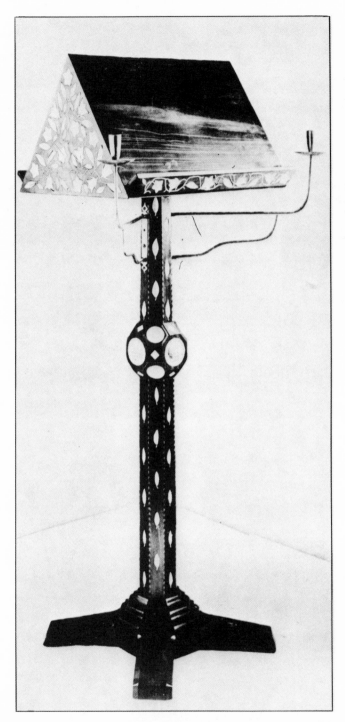
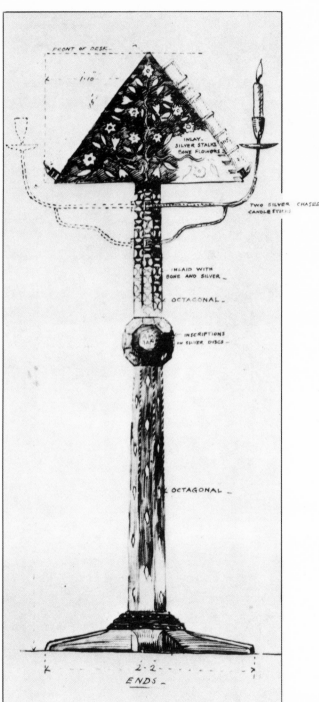

A LECTERN

Plate 23

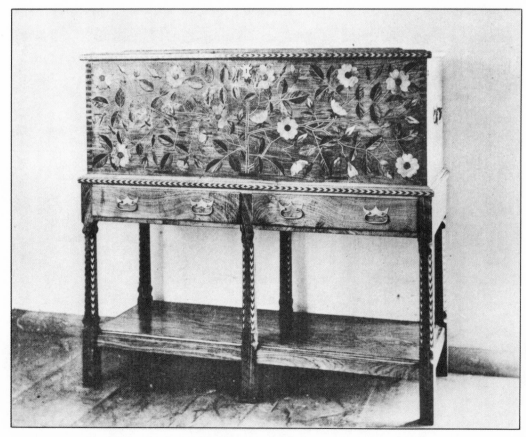

TWO CHESTS

Plate 24

A CABINET

Plate 25

(See notes on Plates for descriptions)

Plate 26

TWO SIDEBOARDS

Plate 27

A WARDROBE

Plate 28

A WRITING CABINET

Plate 29

A CABINET

Plate 30

TWO TABLES

Plate 31

TWO TABLES

Plate 32

TWO TABLES

Plate 33

A CLERGY SEAT

Plate 34

1. FURNITURE FOR KHARTOUM CATHEDRAL

2. STALLS IN ST. ANDREW'S CHAPEL, WESTMINSTER CATHEDRAL

Plate 35

CHURCH FURNITURE

Plate 36

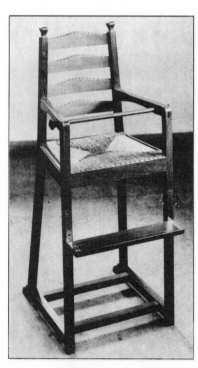

CHAIRS

Plate 37

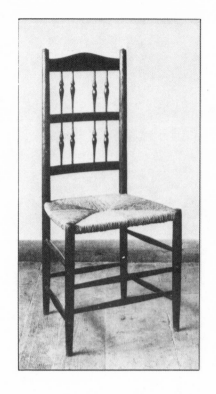

CHAIRS

Plate 38

**A SETTEE AND CHAIRS**

Plate 39

INLAID BOXES

Plate 40

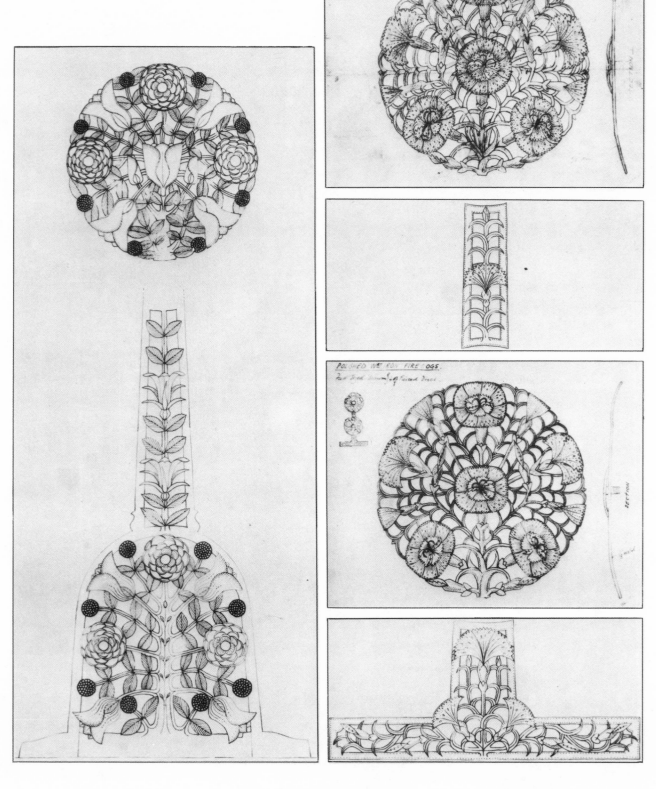

TWO PAIRS OF FIREDOGS

Plate 41

A PAIR OF FIREDOGS

Plate 42

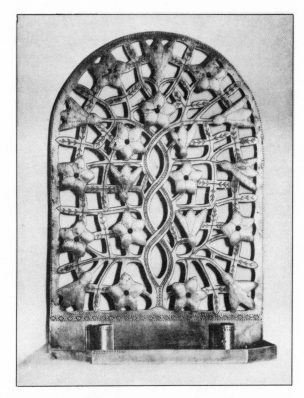

CANDLE SCONCES AND FIREDOGS

Plate 43

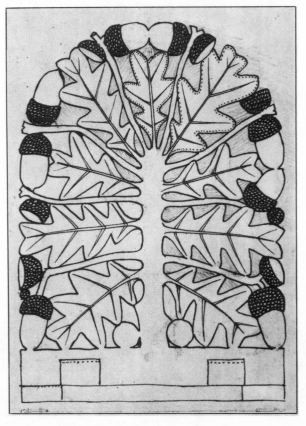

WORKING DRAWINGS FOR SCONCES

Plate 44

WORKING DRAWINGS FOR SCONCES

Plate 45

WORKING DRAWINGS FOR SCONCES

Plate 46

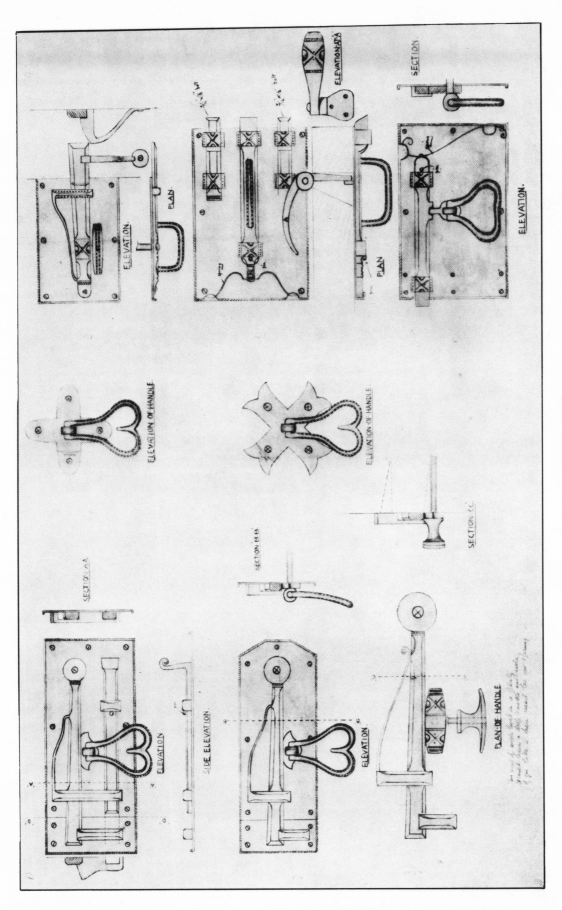

DOOR FURNITURE

Plate 47

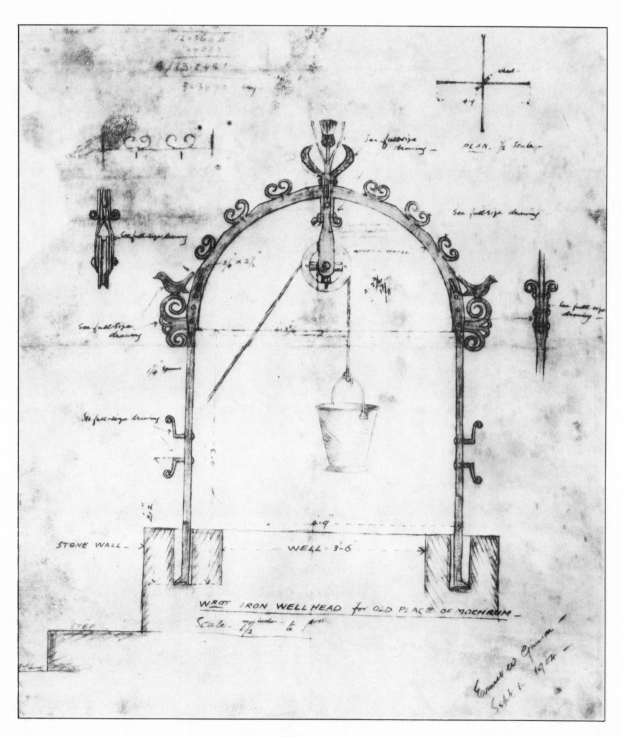

A WELL HEAD

Plate 48

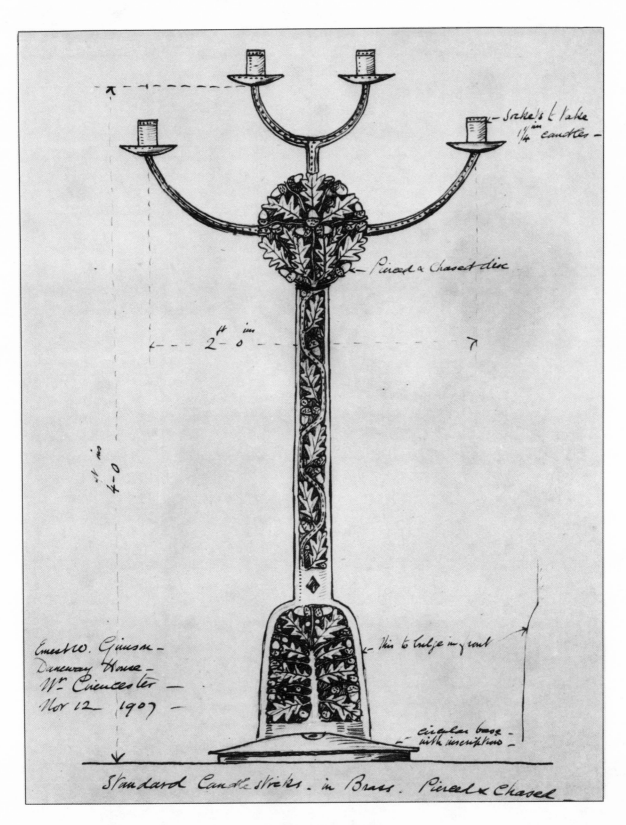

Sockets to take 1¼ᵢₙ candles

Pierced & Chased disc

2ft 0in

4ft 0in

Ernest W. Gimson —
Daneway House —
Nr Cirencester —
Nov 12 1907 —

this to bulge in front

circular base
with inscription

Standard Candlesticks. in Brass. Pierced & Chased

**ALTAR CANDLESTICKS**

Plate 49

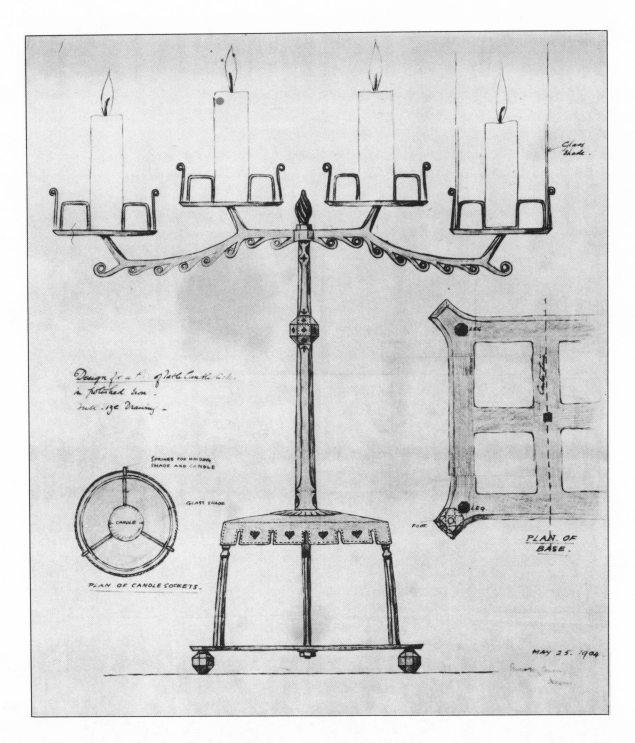

Glass
Shade.

Design for a pair of Table Candlesticks.
in polished Iron.
full size Drawing.

SPRINGS FOR HOLDING
SHADE AND CANDLE

GLASS SHADE

CANDLE

PLAN OF CANDLE SOCKETS.

LEG

Candles

LEG.

FOOT.

PLAN OF
BASE.

MAY 25. 1904.

**A PAIR OF TABLE CANDLESTICKS**

Plate 50

1. A WEATHERCOCK

2. A FIREGUARD

Plate 51

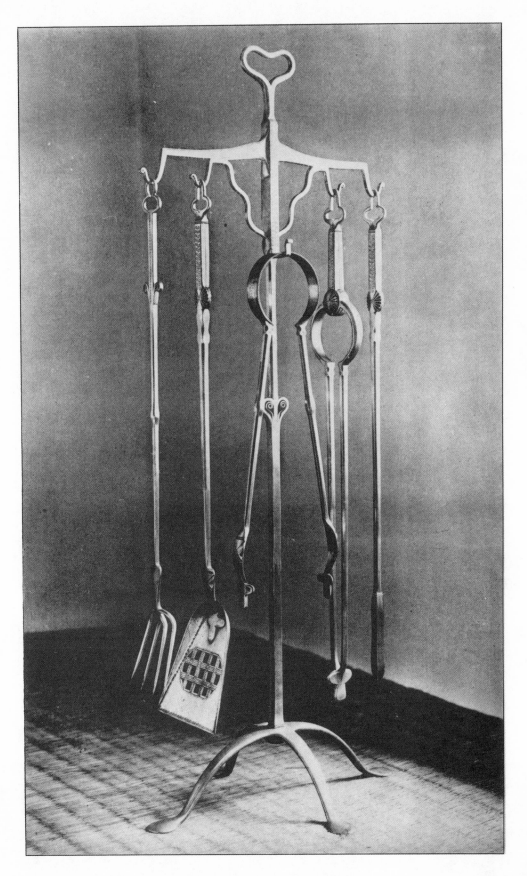

A STAND OF FIRE-IRONS

Plate 52

AN ALTAR CROSS

Plate 53

TWO CEILINGS IN MODELLED PLASTERWORK

Plate 54

INTERIOR OF A ROOM AT PINBURY PARK

Plate 55

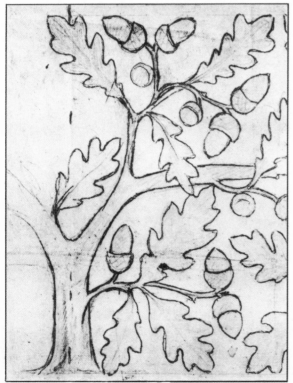

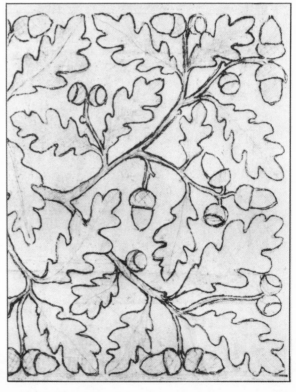

CARVING ON MANTELPIECE SHEWN ON Plate 54

Plate 56

AN EMBROIDERED HANGING

Plate 57

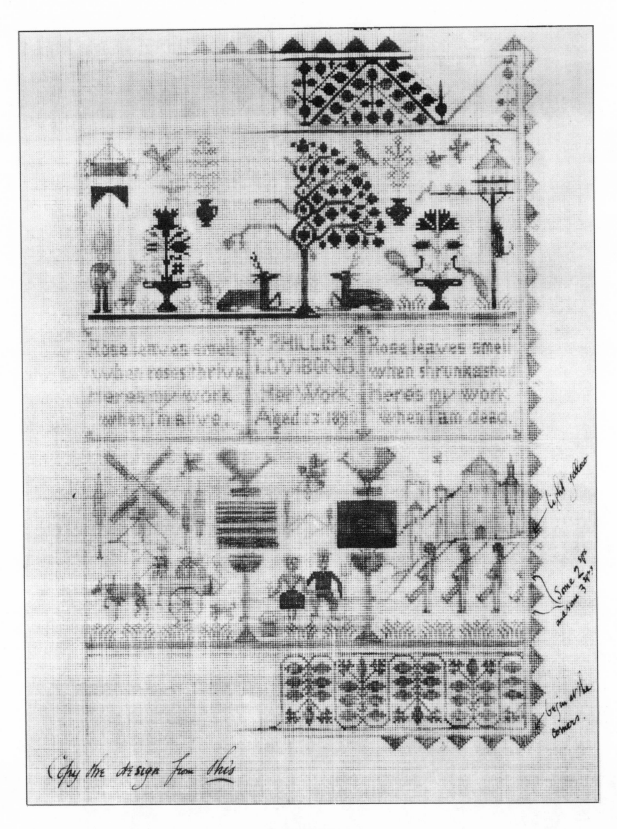

A SAMPLER

Plate 58

A LEATHER BOOK-BINDING

Plate 59

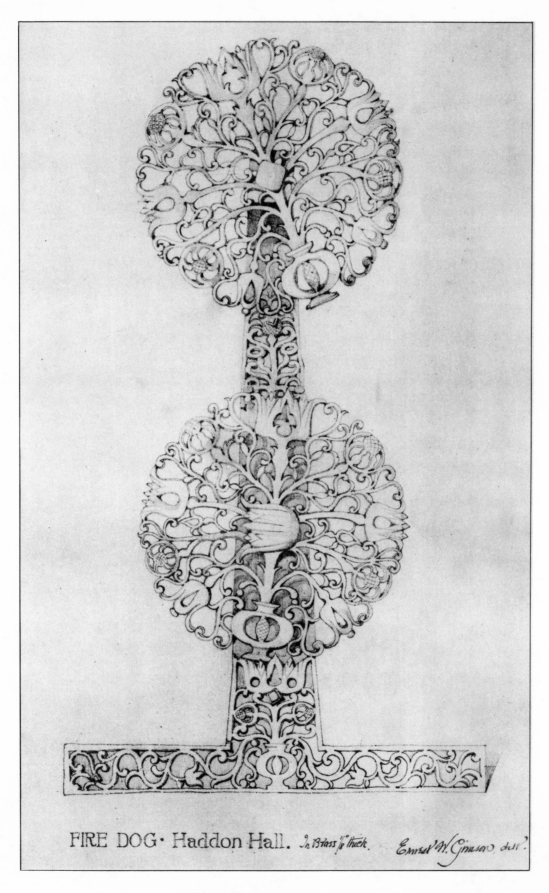

FIRE DOG· Haddon Hall. *In Brass ⅛" thick.* *Ernest W. Gimson, del.*

A DRAWING BY ERNEST GIMSON

Plate 60

TWO DRAWINGS BY ERNEST GIMSON

# A LIST OF THE
# Original Subscribers

EDWARD ADLARD, J.P., Postlip, Winchcombe
Russell Alexander, 43 Old Town, Clapham, S.W.
J. A. O. Allan, F.R.I.B.A., 25 Union Terrace, Aberdeen
Joseph Armitage, 61 Eagle Street, W.C.1
Charles M. C. Armstrong, F.R.I.B.A., Warwick
Mrs Hubert Astley, Brinsop Court, Herefordshire
Herbert Baker, 14 Barton Street, S.W.1
Geoffrey M. Bark, 147 Leam Terrace, Leamington Spa
Edward Barnsley, Froxfield, Petersfield, Hants. *Two copies*
A. Ernest Barnsley, Sapperton, Cirencester
Sidney H. Barnsley, Sapperton, Cirencester. *Two copies*
The Earl Bathurst, Cirencester Park, Cirencester
The Librarian, Bedales, Petersfield
Mrs I. Bedford, Lake View, Vale of Health, Hampstead, N.W.3
Constance M. Belliss, at Bradbourne Hall, Ashbourne, Derbyshire
R. A. Berkeley, Fir Wood, Chesterton, Cirencester
The Hon. Claude Biddulph, Rodmarton, Cirencester
The Library, Central School of Arts and Crafts, Margaret Street,
    Birmingham
Detmar Blow, Hilles House, Painswick, Glos.
Mrs Jellings Blow, Turville Heath, Henley-on-Thames
The School of Arts & Crafts, Bradford
Walter H. Brierley, F.S.A., F.R.I.B.A., 13 Lendal, York
John & Edward Bumpus, Ltd, 350 Oxford Street, W.1
Walter R. Butler, 84 William Street, Melbourne, Australia. *Three
    copies*
Paul S. Cadbury, Hillcrest, Farquhar Road, Edgbaston,
    Birmingham
W. A. Cadbury, Suffolk House, Cheltenham

The Original Subscribers

The Library of Charterhouse School, Godalming
D. W. Herdman, Librarian, Cheltenham Public Library, Art Gallery & Museum, Cheltenham
The Chicago Public Library, Chicago, Ill., U.S.A.
Arthur F. Collins, The University College of Southampton
J. Paul Cooper, Betsom's Hill, Westerham, Kent
The Cotswold Gallery, 59 Frith Street, Soho Square, W.1
The Earl of Crawford and Balcarres, 7 Audley Square, W.1
The late Theodore Crewdson, Styal, Handforth, Cheshire
Stanley W. Davies, New Road, Windermere
F. J. Dryhurst, C.B., 8 Sheffield Terrace, Kensington, W.8
Eason & Son, Ltd, Dublin
Marie L. Eckhard, Piper's Plot, Lockeridge, Marlborough
Hugh C. Fairfax-Cholmeley, Brandsby, York
The Earl Ferrers, Staunton Harold, Ashby-de-la-Zouch. *Three copies*
B. J. Fletcher, Central School of Arts & Crafts, Margaret Street, Birmingham.
W. & G. Foyle, Ltd, 121-125 Charing Cross Road, W.C.2. *Three copies*
Edward G. H. Gardiner, 5 Sherbourne Terrace, Leamington Spa
MacDonald Gill, 1 Hare Court, Temple, E.C.4
Arthur Gimson, Rhoscolyn, Toller Road, Leicester
Basil L. Gimson, Five Oaks, Steep, Petersfield
Harold Gimson, White House, Clarendon Park, Leicester. *Six copies*
Herbert Gimson, 46 Ladbrooke Square, W.11
J. M. Gimson, 108 Regent Road, Leicester. *Three copies*
J. R. Gimson, 90 Sparkenhoe Street, Leicester. *Two copies*
K. S. Gimson, Stonygate House, Toller Road, Leicester
Margaret Gimson, 4 Belmont Villas, New Walk, Leicester
Sydney A. Gimson, 20 Glebe Street, Leicester. *Five copies*
Mrs T. W. Gimson, Sunnyfield, Newcastle, Staffs.
James P. Halcrow, Librarian, The Glasgow School of Art, 167 Renfrew Street, Glasgow

ij

Nancie Gorton, The Sesame Shop, Stroud

T. F. W. Grant, M.C., F.R.I.B.A., 11 Buckingham Street,
   Adelphi, W.C.2

Sidney K. Greenslade, 10 Powderham Crescent, Exeter

F. L. Griggs, A.R.A., Campden, Glos.

Arthur Grove, 1 Hare Court, Temple, E.C.4

G. F. B. de Gruchy, Manoir de Noirmont, Jersey

W. S. Hadaway, School of Arts, Madras

Joan Harvey & Elizabeth Woodard, Orchard Close, Britwell
   Salome, Watlington, Oxon.

Ambrose Heal, Baylin's Farm, Beaconsfield

Heal & Son, Ltd, 196 Tottenham Court Road, W.1

Mrs de la Hey, North Cerney Rectory, Cirencester

A. D. Hislop, 124 St Vincent Street, Glasgow

Laurence W. Hodson, Bradbourne Hall, Ashbourne, Derbyshire

P. Morley Horder, 5 Arlington Street, St. James', S.W.1

C. H. St J. Hornby, Shelley House, Chelsea Embankment, S.W.3

H. G. Ibberson, The Gables, Hunstanton

A. L. Irvine, Lord's Meade, Godalming

Alfred James, Edgeworth Manor, Cirencester

Norman Jewson, Sapperton, Cirencester. *Three copies*

P. W. Jewson, The Lindens, Lime-Tree Road, Norwich

Thomas Jones, 2 Whitehall Gardens, S.W.1

Canon R. Charles S. Jones, Fairford Vicarage, Glos.

J. T. Jordan, The School of Art, Newcastle, Staffs.

Mrs Sickenga Knappert, 35 Singel Bde R., Dordrecht, Holland

H. G. Malcolm Laing, 9 Old Square, Lincoln's Inn, W.C.2

The Leicester and Leicestershire Society of Architects, Leicester

Mrs F. Lefroy, 407 Merton Street, Toronto, Canada

W. R. Lethaby, 111 Inverness Terrace, W2

Asa Lingard, The Ryddings, Emm Lane, Bradford

The London County Council, per F. W. Mackinney, Chief Officer
   of Stores

Ellen Lovibond, 20 Glebe Street, Leicester. *Two copies*

Geoffrey H. Lupton, Froxfield, Petersfield. *Two copies*

The Original
Subscribers
Wilfrid Mathieson, Minchinhampton, Glos.
Bache Matthews, The Birmingham Repertory Theatre,
 Birmingham
T. McMeekan, Water Lane House, Stroud, Glos.
Mrs Theodosia Middlemore, Melsetter, Orkney
G. Ll. Morris, Swan Cottage, Ridgeview Road, Whetstone, N.20
May Morris, Kelmscott Manor, Lechlade, Glos.
Basil Mott, 10 Arkwright Road, Hampstead, N.W.3
B. H. Newdigate, St Brigid's, Stratford-upon-Avon
The Municipal School of Art, Nottingham, per J. Else, Principal
Basil Oliver, 148 Kensington High Street, W.8
Barry Parker, J.P., F.R.I.B.A., Norton Way, Letchworth. *Two
 copies*
Harry H. Peach, Dryad Works, Leicester. *Two copies*
Arthur J. Penty, 66 Strand on Green, Chiswick, W.4
Alfred H. Powell, 40 Mecklenburgh Square, W.C.1
Oliver Powell, Charity Farm, Horsham Road, Sussex
A. R. Powys, 13 Hammersmith Terrace, W.6
R. Ll. B. Rathbone, 3 Ravenscourt Square, W.6
Russell & Sons, Lygon Cottage, Broadway, Worcestershire
Charles Rutherston, 11 Park Drive, Heaton, Bradford
A. I. Schué, 16 Hobart Place, S.W.1
Prof. Allen W. Seaby, University College, Reading
J. Henry Sellers, 78 King Street, Manchester
H. P. Shapland, A.R.I.B.A., 29 Hornsey Lane, Highgate, N.6
Eric Sharpe, Old Brewery Cottage, Stanpit, Christchurch, Hants.
W. G. Simmonds, The Frith, Far Oakridge, Stroud, Glos.
Hubert W. Simpson, The Handicrafts, Kendal
A. Dunbar Smith, 6 Queen's Square, Bloomsbury, W.C.1
Mrs Bernhard Smith, XXI Gallery, Adelphi, W.C.2
Hamilton T. Smith, 10 St John's Wood Road, N.W.6
Charles Spooner, Eyot Cottage, Chiswick Mall, W.
Sir Charles Stewart Wilson, K.C.I.E., Gomms Wood, Knotty
 Green, Beaconsfield
Walter Stoye, The Anchorage, Aldenham Road, Bushey, Herts.

John Henry Thomas, Wedderburn House, Wedderburn Road, Hampstead, N.W.3

Isabel C. Thompson, St Helen's School, Northwood, Middlesex. *Two copies*

G. F. Tothill, 123 Pembroke Road, Clifton, Bristol

F. W. Troup, 6 Mandeville Place, W.1. *Two copies*

Laurence A. Turner, F.S.A., 56 Doughty Street, W.C.1

Percy Turner, A.R.I.B.A., 23 Bank Street, Bradford

Thackeray Turner, F.S.A., Westbrook, Godalming

The Victoria & Albert Museum, South Kensington, S.W.7

P. Vander Waals, Chestnut House, Chalford, Glos. *Five copies*

The National Library of Wales, per John Ballinger, Librarian

Emery Walker, 16 Clifford's Inn, E.C.4

R. G. Walker, 16 The Avenue, Bedford Park, W.4

Sir Lawrence Weaver, K.B.E., F.S.A., 38 Hamilton Terrace, N.W.8

Stanley J. Wearing, A.R.I.B.A., 3 Redwell Street, Norwich

J. T. Webster, Shallowford House, near Stone, Staffs.

Robert W. S. Weir, The Barn, Hartley Wintney, Basingstoke, Hants.

William Weir, Meadow House, Cobham, Kent

A. Randall Wells, Slinfold Manor, Sussex

Charles Wells, 134 Cromwell Road, St Andrew's Park, Bristol

C. W. Whall, 37 Harvard Road, Gunnersbury, W.4

C. H. Whitaker, 313 East 23rd Street, New York City, New York

W. E. Wilkinson, Springfield College, Wake Green Road, Moseley, Birmingham

Charles C. Winmill, 2 Eliot Place, Blackheath, Kent

Percy & Mary Withers, Souldern Court, Banbury

Helen Wootton, 19 Rotton Park Road, Edgbaston, Birmingham

J. Hubert Worthington, 178 Oxford Road, Manchester

John Williams, Principal, Hammersmith School of Arts & Crafts, W.12

G. B. Young, Kilmington, Axminster